Advance praise for

Rich in scriptural truth, *We...* your faith by pointing you to Christ. Dave Perry has a knack for describing old truths in new ways through his powerful use of language, vivid imagery, biblical connections that you hadn't thought of before, and application to life today. This book will help you to keep going back to the treasure within, even—especially—when life is tough.

—Mike Beaumont
UK Pastor, Professor, Author, Broadcaster

The wearied and worried will find encouragement in these pages.

—Andrew Micklefield
Manitoba MLA, Rossmere

Dave Perry has given us superb reflections on scripture. I wish I saw what he sees! The treasure he finds in God's Word is amazing in its depth.

—Steve Thomas
International Team Leader for Salt & Light Ministries

This book is treasure indeed ... treasure for every day. It has been mined from years of experience by a theologian with the gifts of humility, honesty, and imaginative insights. A book to treasure that will enrich your life!

—David Freeman
Director, Highlight Teacher Training, England

Whenever Dave Perry came as a visiting lecturer to King's Bible College, he was loved for his humour and fresh insights, his love for the Bible and—on a separate shelf—*The Lord of the Rings!* This selection of short meditations reflects those same qualities: sharing fresh insights across the whole range of scripture and rooted in everyday life. A forty-day spiritual workout!

—Tony Gray
Former Principal, King's Bible College, Scotland

Dave Perry masterfully reminds us that our theology of treasure will impact every aspect of our lives. Weaving together biblical truths and personal stories, he encourages us to better understand our treasure and recognize that, in the end, all will be well because of "God's faithful, enabling presence."

—Elizabeth Mittelstadt
Long-time Teacher and Life-long Learner
Winnipeg

This collection of meditations is encouraging, relatable, convicting, and comforting. Each piece is full of thought-provoking revelations. I found myself scribbling notes and repeating certain lines three or four times just to let their profound truths sink in. In a time of loss and grief on a global scale—Covid 19—David reminds us of the hope we have in our Treasure: Christ.

—Bethany MacLean
Teacher, Winnipeg

We Have This Treasure

Meditations for Jars-of-Clay People

To Raj & Kim, with our thanks for all you've done to care for and support Lucy.

Pete & Julia

May 29, 2022

David Perry

Foreword by Gus Konkel

WE HAVE THIS TREASURE
Copyright © 2021 by David Perry

Printed in Canada

Print ISBN: 978-1-4866-2115-6 | eBook ISBN: 978-1-4866-2116-3

Word Alive Press
119 De Baets Street, Winnipeg, MB R2J 3R9
www.wordalivepress.ca

Cataloguing in Publication may be obtained through Library and Archives Canada

To David Freeman, who has strengthened my hand in God
(1 Samuel 23:16).

Contents

The Treasure
We're All Seeking

This book leads you to the treasure desperately needed by the church—and the world—today. The suffering and mystified man, Job, searched for such a treasure. In the masterful poem of Job 28, he reflected on how people know the way to gold and sapphires, even in the depths of the earth. But Job had a question: Who knew the way to *wisdom* (the ultimate treasure)? Answer: Only God! God in mercy comes to this world to reveal this treasure. Paul said:

> *But we impart a secret and hidden wisdom of God, which God decreed before the ages for our glory ... 'What no eye has seen, nor ear heard, nor the heart of man imagined, what God has prepared for those who love him."*

—I Corinthians 2:7, 9

In a second letter to the Corinthians, Paul spoke of this treasure as being stored in clay jars. You are holding such an earthen jar. Here is an example of the treasure we need: the instruction of a wise teacher, the kind of teacher who has himself followed a lifetime of listening to wisdom and acquiring instruction (Proverbs 1:5). This book is a guide to direct the reader on the right path, to learn trust and the confidence of knowing the will of the Lord in all manner of circumstance, to learn the humility that is the foundation of joy. So enjoy and learn from this book. These meditations are one means of acquiring the treasure of living the joy of our salvation in Christ Jesus.

August H. Konkel

McMaster Divinity College, 2021

Introduction

What These Meditations Aim to Do—And How They Aim to Do It

The forty devotionals that follow aim to help us meditate on a specific theme in Scripture. By meditate, I mean to soak our thoughts and think deeply and slowly, which is what Psalm 1 says to do with God's written Word. The theme can be found in 2 Corinthians 4:7a: *"But we have this treasure in jars of clay."* The meditations lead us to ponder how selected passages in both Testaments develop this central idea.

The meditations are brief—around four to five hundred words each. You won't read far before you come across something Bible scholars call "bookends." Bookends are matching truths the biblical writers set at the start and finish of a book, or a section within a book. The match-up becomes part of the message, like in Matthew 1:23 (the meaning of "Immanuel") and Matthew 28:20 (the "I am with you always" promise). Beginning and end, God, in Christ, is with us. That truth is key to Matthew's message. That is bookending.

We Have This Treasure is an archive of thoughts from my Facebook page, "Dave's Posts." The posts were written over a span of six years. Ideas already used on Facebook got brought back onto the bus, sometimes many months later. Two consecutive meditations in this book may have been born as Facebook posts three years apart. ("Bookending" is one of those.) I've made an editorial decision to leave these re-inclusions in place, so you'll meet the same passengers more than once.

I refer to other books along with the Bible in the meditations. One is Tolkien's *The Lord of the Rings* (multiple references to that one).[1] But another book impacted me as a boy and represents what I hope this book will be to people. Today, at age seventy, I can recall curling up on my parents' sofa with a book. I was around ten years old, and the book was a children's edition of *The Count of Monte Cristo* by Alexandre Dumas. I came to the pivotal "Edmond finds the treasure" scene—and was captivated. Through a written document that required careful interpretation (sound familiar?), Edmond Dantès found a vast hidden trove of gold coins and priceless jewels—wealth beyond the riches of kings. It went beyond Edmond's imagination and filled him with wonder. And what lingered in my schoolboy mind wasn't Dumas's account of the trove's gold but his description of Edmond's wonder.[2]

That image still lingers, and it points me to Scripture: "*I rejoice in your word like one who discovers a great treasure*" (Psalm

119:162, NLT). God's written Word as a treasure. Now, grandfather age, I'm still learning to delight in running my hands through that gold.

May this little book enable you to do the same.

David Perry

Winnipeg

January 2021

The Apostle Paul's Theology of Treasure

The apostle Paul had a clear theology of treasure:

> *For God, who said, "Let light shine out of darkness," has shone in our hearts to give the light of the knowledge of the glory of God in the face of Jesus Christ. But we have this treasure in jars of clay, to show that the surpassing power belongs to God and not to us. We are afflicted in every way, but not crushed; perplexed, but not driven to despair; persecuted, but not forsaken; struck down, but not destroyed; always carrying in the body the death of Jesus, so that the life of Jesus may also be manifested in our bodies.*
>
> —2 Corinthians 4:6–10

Treasure theology, Part One: What the treasure was: "... *the knowledge of the glory of God in the face of Jesus Christ.*" Israel knew God's glory in his manifest presence in the tabernacle (Exodus 40:38). That, and not the abundant gold in the Holy of Holies, was their treasure. Paul taught that the church knew the same glory but in a different way—not in a fire-crowned tent but in a knowable person, Jesus Christ. Knowing him was the treasure.

Part Two: Where the treasure was: Today the US government stores its gold in Fort Knox: an electric-fenced, concrete and steel fortress next door to an army base. But God, said Paul, stores his treasure in jars of clay. Clay: moistened, molded dust: ordinary, unglamourous stuff.[3] Why? To show that it wasn't about the jars. It was about the treasure.

Part Three: What the treasure did: It enabled. The treasure that dungeon-escapee Edmond Dantès found on the island of Monte Cristo enabled him to wield influence and pursue justice.[4] The riches Christians find in Christ enable them to face life at its worst and push through: *"We are afflicted in every way, but not crushed ..."* How? By knowing God's glory in Christ—the enabling treasure.

Part Four: When the treasure came to people: Speaking of the renewing of our bodies at the Last Day, Paul said, *"... we shall all be changed"* (I Corinthians 15:51b). Notice that he used the future-tense verb *"shall ... be changed."* We eagerly wait—even groan—for that day (Romans 8:23). When speaking of knowing God's glory in Christ, however, Paul used the present tense: *"We have this treasure."* Today. Now—in our most jars-of-clay moments—we know him. For Paul, that was the treasure.

One

"Yayyy!"

". . . the trees . . . shall clap their hands."

—Isaiah 55:12b

My friend Keith often prays, "Yayyy!" It's a prayer like a cheer—what you do when your team scores a goal. It's a good prayer because it echoes what heaven continuously does for Christ: it cheers.

Think back: God set a star in the sky to herald Jesus' arrival on earth: a cosmic "Yayyy!" (Matthew 2:2). A choir of angels arrived to cheer for the same event, singing, *"Glory to God in the highest!"* (Luke 2:14a). "Yayyy" again.

More cheers followed. The transfiguration: a "Yayyy" that clothed Christ with light and said, *"This is my beloved Son"* (Matthew 17:5b). The resurrection: a "Yayyy" that raised Christ from the dead. And don't miss that dramatic flourish of the angel rolling back the stone and *sitting* on it—yes (Matthew 28:2)! Death was defeated, and heaven was cheering.

Even these scenes don't exhaust the Bible's "Yayyys!" The biggest of all actually appeared in Psalm 24, some one thousand years before Christ came to earth. It prophetically described the angels cheering for Jesus as he re-entered heaven: *"Lift up your heads, O gates! And be lifted up, O ancient doors, that the King of glory may come in. Who is this King of glory? The Lord, strong and mighty, the Lord, mighty in battle!"* (Psalm 24:7—8).

In their original setting, these words acted as a cheer for Yahweh, the warrior king, likely at his entrance into Jerusalem with the ark of the covenant (1 Chronicles 13, 15–16; Psalms 68,132).[5] The people hailed him as "mighty in battle." He was the one who took on gods (Exodus 12:12), kings (Exodus 14:18), and seas (Exodus 14:29)—and won. But post-resurrection eyes can also see Christ here as the ultimate warrior king. He took on Satan (John 12:31), sin (Romans 6:4) and death (2 Timothy 1:10)—and won. He was mighty in battle. When he rose again and ascended into heaven, heaven cheered: *"Lift up your heads, O gates!"*[6]

Imagine standing outside a stadium where your hometown team is in a playoff game. You don't know the score, but you know the game must be nearly over. The outcome matters to you. Then you hear an explosive and sustained roar. The crowd is wildly cheering. Your team has won, and your emotions lift. You yell out, "Yayyy!"

The apostle John wrote, *"And I heard every creature in heaven and on earth and under the earth and in the sea ... saying, 'To him who sits on the throne and to the Lamb be ... glory ... forever and ever!'"* (Revelation 5:13). What did John hear? Cheering. Cheering that lifted and enabled. That is the treasure.

Two

The Single
Self-Replenishing Source

"... the water I ... give ... will become ... a spring ..."
—John 4:14

One day in the late 1950s, my grandfather was negotiating the purchase of a field in rural Vermont. He wanted to build a vacation home and had seen a For Sale sign on a plot of land. The owner of the land was Charlie Foster. Henry Perry went to see him.

Charlie was a farmer looking to sell a corner of his property he no longer needed. In true Vermont form, he was a man of few words. Why use sentences when a word will do? The halting conversation turned to the subject of a spring on the property, which my grandfather wanted to use as a water-source for his planned house.

"Has the spring ever run dry?" he asked Charlie.

Charlie removed his pipe from his mouth. "Nope." He put the pipe back in his mouth.

"Can you guarantee it won't run dry?"

Pipe out. "Nope." Pipe back in.

Negotiation, Vermont style.

Charlie was simply stating the facts. Springs are all ultimately rain dependent. They don't self-replenish—with one exception. Christ told the woman at the well, "... *whoever drinks of the water that I will give him will never be thirsty again. The water that I will give him will become in him a spring of water welling up to eternal life*" (John 4:14). Water that would become a spring! It wouldn't need to be replenished because it would self-replenish. It would be its own source. Not in a Vermont field, but inside "whoever drinks". It *"will become in him a spring of water."*

In him? In the man who finds out his three-year-old daughter has cancer? A self-replenishing spring in *him*? Yes.

In her? In the confused teenager whose boyfriend is pressuring her for sex? A self-replenishing spring in *her*? Yes.

In them? In the Latin American Christians whose pastor preached last Sunday against the local drug lords, and who on Wednesday night saw their new building levelled by arson? A self-replenishing spring in *them*? Yes.

The water Christ gives us doesn't make us numb. We will still face dismay and confusion and grief—things that are *"common to man"* (I Corinthians 10:13). The water isn't an anesthetic. It is water, but water of the very best kind: internal (*"in him"*), sustaining (*"never be thirsty"*), and self-replenishing (*"a spring ... welling up"*).

Can a Vermont farm field give us that kind of water? Nope. But Christ can. That's why knowing him is the treasure.

Three

People with Baggage

"I will send survivors . . ."

—Isaiah 66:19a

Books of the Bible, like most books, have clear and intentional beginnings and endings. In some cases, the writers verbally linked them by using matching words or corresponding ideas in the opening and closing passages. This technique is called bookending, and it is a deliberate pointer to the book's message. Often the bookends match: Matthew began and ended his gospel with the "God with us" promise (see 1:23 and 28:20). But sometimes the bookends form a contrast (like darkness and light).

We find an example of contrastive bookending in Isaiah. Isaiah opened his book with a grim picture of Jerusalem's apostasy. He used descriptions any healthcare worker will know all too well: *"From the sole of the foot even to the head, there is no soundness … [only] bruises and sores and raw wounds…"* (1:6a). Raw wounds. *"Putrefying sores"* in the KJV. Not very nice. That was the front bookend.

At the end of the book, he wrote the concluding bookend: a picture of Jerusalem restored. Instead of a people with oozing lesions, we see a city sending out heralds of God's glory. God declared: *"… I will send survivors to the nations … And they shall declare my glory among the nations"* (66:19). From people with putrefying sores to an army on a mission—the contrast could not be more dramatic. And that is what God promised.

I just called these people an army, and they will be, but they will be an army that marches in weakness. Whom did God say he would send? *"Survivors."* Survivors from sin-sickness (remember the lesion-scarred people of Isaiah 1). Survivors from exile: so weak the Shepherd had to carry them home (Isaiah 40:11). And today, survivors from damaged childhoods, marriage bust-ups, church splits, pornography addictions, and seasons in the younger son's *"distant country"* (Luke 15:13, NIV). And survivors of calamity, like Paul's famous shipwreck in Acts 27.

Survivors: People who, Jacob-like, limped (Genesis 32:31). Not self-assured, take-life-in-stride types, but people with baggage: *"… conflicts on the outside, [and] fears within"* (2 Corinthians 7:5b, NIV). And God—just because he's

God—sends them anyway. And they go and declare his glory—that is, they tell others about the treasure.

If your raw wounds feel all-too recent, or if you're still traumatized by a shipwreck (Maybe you caused it yourself?), then hold on to the God of Isaiah. Remember his promise to the nations.

And remember whom he said he would send.

Four

The Same Fire

"... fire out of the midst of a bush"

—Exodus 3:2a

Question: What do these seven scenes from Scripture have in common?

- Abram's torch-dream (Genesis 15:17)
- The burning bush (Exodus 3:2)
- God leading refugee Israel in the darkness (Exodus 13:21; Psalm 105:39)
- God's visible presence at Mount Sinai (Exodus 19:18)
- The tabernacle (especially at night) (Exodus 40:38)
- The dedication ceremony for Solomon's temple (2 Chronicles 7:1)
- The day of Pentecost (Acts 2:3)

The common image, of course, is fire—God's presence in the form of flame.

From Abram's torch-dream to the Day of Pentecost—seven scenes out of seven—it was fire. And (note well!) it was the same fire. The fire in the temple was the fire from Sinai, which was the fire from the bush. The faithful, enabling presence of God: scenes in a single story.

Those first six fire-moments (torch-dream to Solomon's temple) were a lead-up, a drum-roll, heralding the real goal in scene seven: God coming to dwell not in torches, bushes, mountains, or temples, but in *people*: "*And divided tongues as of fire appeared to them and rested on each one of them. And they were all filled with the Holy Spirit and began to speak in other tongues as the Spirit gave them utterance*" (Acts 2:3–4). They began to learn to live in a strength that wasn't theirs, to "*walk by the Spirit*" (Romans 8:4; Galatians 5:16). An uphill path? Yes … but walkable because the fire was in them.

They needed all the help they could get. They faced fierce opposition from Jews and Gentiles alike (Acts 13:50; 2 Timothy 4:14). They faced the lingering residue of their own sin (what Paul called "the flesh"): ragged relationships (Acts 6:1; 15:39), moral failures (Acts 5:1–2; 1 John 2:1), and culture gaps—not least of which was between Jewish and Gentile believers (Romans 14):

"Brother, that meat isn't kosher!"

"Kosher? What's that?"

Their mandate? To live pure before God, to think well of one another, and to take the gospel to the ends of the earth. Given their issues, the mission seemed set for failure, except for one fact: God's faithful, enabling presence. They had the fire in them.

If you're a Christian, so do you. Whatever your uphill path at the moment, ponder this: The fire that was in the burning bush is now in you. It's the same fire. It's the treasure.

Five

The God Who
Reversed the Irreversible

". . . the Lord . . . brought the shadow back ten steps . . ."
—2 Kings 20:11

It was 701 B.C., and Hezekiah, King of Judah, was dying. Some were saying, "Look, days come and go; shadows move with the arc of the sun. People get sick, and sometimes they die. Get over it." Their point? Shadows don't go backwards, and terminally ill people don't get better.

But sometimes they do: *"And Isaiah the prophet called to the Lord, and he brought the shadow back ten steps, by which it had gone down on the steps of Ahaz"* (2 Kings 20:11).

If you haven't read 2 Kings 20, spoiler alert: The shadow on the stairway did go backwards—up the stairs, not down. Contrary to experience, observation, history, and the laws of astronomy, it moved backwards up the stairway. And terminally ill King Hezekiah did get better. God granted him an extra fifteen years to live and reign.

Some while ago, two friends of mine went for marriage counselling. "Walls between us," he told me. "It felt beyond repair." However, they believed in—they treasured—the God of 2 Kings: the God who reversed the irreversible. Recall:

2 Kings 4:1–7: He enacted a financial rescue of two young boys from debt-slavery. In those days, rescue from debt-slavery didn't happen. It just didn't happen.

2 Kings 6:1–6: He made a lost, sunk-in-the-river axe head float to the surface. (Question for any grade-school science class: does iron float?)

2 Kings 13:21: He made a dead man—newly lowered into a community tomb—come back to life.

2 Kings 20:9–11: He made the shadow turn backwards and move up the stairway. And he healed a terminally ill king.

Do debt-slaves get set free? Of course not. Does iron float? Of course not.

Do people climb out of their own graves? Of course not. Do shadows on the ground go backwards? Of course not.

Do kings in palliative care recover—and go on to rule nations? No. Do terminally troubled marriages get back on track? No.

But sometimes they do. (My friends' marriage did.)

You may be dealing with a sunken axe head: something that appears irreversibly lost. If so, look to the God of 2 Kings as your treasure. He reversed the irreversible. To him be the glory.

Six

The Dog, the Gramophone, and the Lord of the Storm

"Who then is this . . .?"

—Mark 4:41b

Take a brain-moment and see how many corporate logos you can think of. (By "logos" I mean commercial symbols of companies, like the golden arches). Here are a few: General Electric's circular calligraphic emblem, "GE"; Chrysler's five-pointed star; Jaguar's (surprise!) jaguar; or HMV, with the dog sitting in front of an old-fashioned gramophone, peering into the horn-shaped speaker. Beneath the picture are the words: "His Master's Voice" (hence the initials in the company name). HMV wants us to believe that their products so faithfully reproduce sound that a dog would recognize its owner's recorded voice. It would think, *That's my master!*

"Recognition" happened the day Christ calmed the storm (Mark 4:35–41). The wind and the waves heard Jesus speak

"*Peace! Be still!*" (v. 39b). For all their overwhelming and deadly power, they recognized the Master's voice. We can imagine the sea shouting to the wind:

"Hey, wind! Did you hear that?"

"Hear what? I can't hear anything. We're making too much noise!"

"Well listen! That voice! I know that voice! That's the voice that told all us seas to be gathered together into one place and to let the dry land appear! That's the voice that told us to open up and let the children of Israel pass through! That's the Master's voice!"

The wind listens. It hears the voice. "Yes! You're right! We better settle down!"

"*Then the wind died down and it was completely calm . . .* [And his disciples] *asked each other, 'Who then is this? Even the wind and the waves obey him!'*" (Mark 4:39b, 41, NIV).

Speaking of waves, I recall being eleven years old at the beach and nearly drowning. I was some thirty yards from shore in a rougher-than-I-realized Atlantic Ocean surf. I started to slip under, bob up, and slip under again. My uncle on the beach saw what was up (or rather, down) and ran and swam to my rescue. He was why I'm still here.

The emotion of that moment in my eleven-year-old mind? Raw helplessness. Water—hundreds of pounds of water—pressing in. I was no match for it. Perhaps on that summer day in 1961, "hundreds of pounds of water" was an accurate estimate. Not so for that storm on the Sea of Galilee. That was tons of water—easily enough to sink a boat. But Jesus, unlike my uncle, didn't need to run and swim and grab and pull and swim some more. All he had to do was speak. The winds and the waves knew the Master's voice.

They still do. Knowing that is finding the treasure.

Seven

Spirit-Led in the Wasteland

"I have led you forty years in the wilderness."

—Deuteronomy 29: 5a

Elmer Chen shared with me a gospel-gem from Luke's account of Christ's experience in the desert. It was about a difference in detail between the way Matthew and Mark told the story (which matched) compared to the way Luke told it, which was slightly different. A difference of a single word.

Matthew and Mark reported the Spirit leading Jesus "into" the desert. Newly baptized, he journeyed from the Jordan to the wilderness. He entered it. Hence the matching text of Matthew 4:1 and Mark 1:12: *"into the wilderness"* (note that preposition "into"). It was a Spirit-led entry.

That was Matthew and Mark. But Luke told the story slightly differently. He said Jesus was *"led by the Spirit in the wilderness"* (4:1, emphasis added)—not "into" (*eis*) but "in" (*en*).

The focus for Luke wasn't Jesus' arrival in the desert but the time he spent there. Whatever those forty days looked like for Jesus, they were not aimless or pointless. He was led by the Spirit. In the wasteland, the Spirit led him.

So that was Jesus. Amen twice. But what about us?

Here's why what happened to Jesus was hugely relevant to us: Paul wrote in Romans 8:17 that Christians are heirs of God and co-heirs with Christ. What God did for his Son, he commits to doing for his Son's co-heirs as well. By the Spirit, he took Jesus into the desert. And by the Spirit, he will take us into places, seasons, and tasks—sometimes tough ones: family tensions, job losses, and sick loved ones who don't get better. And by that Spirit, he will lead us while we're there. The pillar of cloud and fire led Israel in their wilderness. And Jesus in his. And he will lead us, in ours.

Knowing that fact and resting in it: that's the treasure.

Eight

Sometimes, Glory Is a Verb

" . . . that . . . you may . . . glory in Christ . . ."
—Philippians 1:26

The first time I gloried I was eighteen years old. I was cycling with my friend down a long, hairpin-turn road in the French Alps. Eventually the road levelled off in a valley and followed a wide stream. Mike and I coasted onto the verge, got off our bikes, propped them against a fence, and stood and gazed.

For the first time in my life, I felt lost in scenic beauty. Several miles away stood a mountain with dark-blue rock slopes half cloaked in snow (in July!). But it was the mountain's size that made me glory. I didn't grow up around mountains. For me, the scene gave new meaning to the word "immense." I started to laugh—not with amusement but with joy, with amazement and a sense of being very small in the face of something very big, even majestic. I didn't know it, but I was glorying. I was delighting in and getting lost in something outside of myself and way, way bigger than me. That's what it means to glory.

The Bible, Old Testament and New, speaks of glorying: "Glory in his holy name; let the hearts of those who seek the Lord rejoice!" (Psalm 105:3); *"Save us, O Lord our God ... that we may ... glory in your praise"* (Psalm 106:47); *"... [we] worship by the Spirit of God and glory in Christ Jesus ..."* (Philippians 3:3).

Why does "glorying" matter? Because it saves us from getting off track. Paul wrote Philippians, in part, to rebut the off-centre, quasi-Christian movement we now call the Judaizers. They claimed that believers (including Gentile believers) needed to supplement faith in Christ with circumcision, rigorous Sabbath observance, and the Leviticus 11 food laws. The idea of "in Christ alone" wasn't on their screen. They failed to reckon with the seismic covenant-shift God caused when he sent Jesus.

Paul's corrective for the Judaizers' error? For the Philippians to glory. To gaze in wonder and delight at something outside of and bigger than themselves and bigger than the latest swirling controversy. To look at something our struggles can never diminish. When we glory in Christ (like Mike and I gloried in that scenery in 1968), good things happen. We regain perspective. Aching muscles cease to matter. Problems cease to matter. They don't disappear, but they lose their power to smother. We breathe, we laugh, and we linger for another long look at the mountain.

For Christians, that mountain is Christ. Our treasure.

Yes, of course, the road awaits. And maybe it's uphill. But if we're glorying in Christ, we'll be ready.

Nine

The Reality that Releases Us to Risk

"But when Simon Peter saw it . . ."

—Luke 5:8a

Standing in the synagogue to read from the prophet Isaiah, Jesus employed the reading to announce why he had come: *"The Spirit of the Lord is upon me ... to proclaim ... recovering of sight to the blind"* (Luke 4:18). Jesus' reading was about more than physical healing for blind people, although it was that (see Luke 7:21).[7] It was about enabling people to physically, emotionally, and spiritually *see*.

Notice what happened soon after the synagogue scene. Jesus boarded Simon Peter's fishing-boat by the shore of the Lake Gennesaret (Luke 5:1–11). Simon was pinch-tired and frustrated after an empty-net all-nighter on the sea. But at Jesus' word, he put out from the shore and let down his nets. Again. Result? A massive haul.

Peter was blown away. He bowed down in the boat and worshipped Jesus. But as striking and spiritually significant as that bowing was, it wasn't the first thing Luke noted Peter doing. Here is Luke's description of the moment: *"But when Simon Peter saw it* (note: He "saw" something), *he fell down at Jesus' knees, saying, 'Depart from me, for I am a sinful man, O Lord'"* (Luke 5:8).

It was like Joseph's brothers falling down before their now-exalted brother (Genesis 50:18). It was also a recognition of Christ's holiness: *"Depart from me, for I am a sinful man."* We read this and recall Isaiah's *"Woe is me!"* moment on beholding God's holiness in the temple (Isaiah 6:5).

In this pivot-point moment in Peter's life, what provoked this striking reaction (kneeling down in a boat)? Once again, Luke said Peter knelt when he *saw* something. Saw what? The fish in the net, surely. Yes, that—but more. Peter saw (and he realized that he saw) fish that obeyed Jesus and swam into that net. That is, he saw Christ's lordship.

I'll presume to read Peter's thoughts: *If Jesus is Lord over the fish in the sea, then he is Lord over creation. If he's Lord of creation, he is Lord over my future.* Result? Peter *"left everything and followed him"* (Luke 5:11b). Peter saw—or was learning to see—that Jesus was Lord. Jesus was doing what he said in the synagogue that he had come to do: open blind eyes. He opened Peter's eyes, and Peter left everything and followed.

"Everything"—livelihood, predictable future, manageable outcomes. Was that a risk? Of course it was a risk.[8] But Peter could risk because he had seen reality: If Jesus could rule the fish in the sea, he could look after Peter on the land. Realizing that truth was finding the treasure.

Ten

Putting on the New Hat— Six Examples of Changing the Way We Think

"You must change your hearts and minds..."
—Mark 1:15b, JBP[9]

" ◆ ◆ ◆ [B e] transformed by the renewal of your mind" said Paul in Romans 12:2. He was speaking about practical, faithful choices in how we respond to life. It wasn't the first time he dealt with this topic in that letter. Earlier, in Romans 8:6, he called us to relinquish one mind-set (*"the flesh's way of thinking"*) and embrace another (*"the Spirit's way of thinking"*).[10] It's like changing hats:

- Wearing the *old* hat, we try to arrange our world to make us feel safe. Wearing the *new* hat, we yield to *God* arranging *his* world to make Christ preeminent (Colossians 1:18).

- Wearing the *old* hat, we (like King Saul) run from the problem and hide in our tent: "Goliath is too big!" Wearing the *new* hat, we (like David) rally ourselves with truth: "Goliath is big, but God is bigger!" And we will reach for our sling.

- Wearing the *old* hat, we love self-pity: "Poor me!" Wearing the *new* hat, we exult in the goodness of God: *"The Lord is my strength and my song"* (Exodus 15:2a).

- Wearing the *old* hat, we resort to sleazy, toxic ways to comfort ourselves: Pseudo-intimacy in trashy romance novels. Pornography. Wouldn't-that-be-nice fantasies. Wearing the *new* hat, we follow Peter, James, and John up the Mount of Transfiguration and into the glory-cloud (Luke 9:28–35). We stand face-to-face with Christ in true intimacy that pulls us out of ourselves, toward him, and fills us with wonder.

- Wearing the *old* hat, we think our failures are the end. We, like post-denials Peter, weep bitterly (Matthew 26:75). The door to a hopeful future seems bolted shut. Wearing the *new* hat, we realize that by rising again, Jesus enabled us to begin again. And again. And again …

- Wearing the *old* hat, we're like the women arriving, spice-laden, at Christ's tomb. We live life expecting to find a corpse. Our outlook is that Caiaphas is unchallengeable, and change is impossible. Wearing the *new* hat, we're like the women running *from* the tomb with the news that Christ had risen and that *nothing* is impossible (Matthew 28:8).

Moment by moment, how do we keep connected with the treasure? By wearing the new hat.

Eleven

Our Fears, Christ's Signs

"... if you confess with your mouth that Jesus is Lord ..."
—Romans 10:9

The last seven days of Jesus' earthly mission—traditionally called Holy Week—were full of fears and signs. In Mark 10:32, the crowds following Christ on the road to Jerusalem *"were afraid."* Jesus had enemies in Jerusalem (Mark 3:22, 7:1–2, 11:27–29; John 9:22). He himself had made predictions about suffering and death awaiting him (Mark 8:31, 9:91, 10:33). So fear was in the air.

But for those who had eyes to see, there were also signs. Signs that as Jesus headed into danger, he was no hapless victim. He was Lord. He was Lord of hostile Jerusalem just as much as he had been Lord over the stormy sea. He gave two signs of that lordship. Neither were public attention-getters, but both showed what the church would later confess as its gospel and its battle-cry: "Jesus is Lord."

The first sign took place on Sunday—Palm Sunday— just prior to the triumphal entry. Jesus sent two disciples to a nearby village to fetch a colt. He simply said, "... *you will find a colt tied* ..." (Mark 11:2). So they went and (surprise!) "*they found a colt tied*" (Mark 11:4). He even predicted the brief dialogue the two would have with the people noticing them untying the animal (Mark 11:5).

Do we have eyes to see? It was a sign: "They found a colt tied." A sign that amid hovering danger and seemingly out-of-control circumstances, Jesus had things in hand. He was Lord.

The second sign came four days later: "*And he sent two of his disciples* ... [saying] *'Go into the city, and a man carrying a jar of water will meet you* ... [and] *he will show you a large upper room'*... *And the disciples set out and found it just as he had told them* ..." (Mark 14:13–16a). Note well those words: "just as he had told them." Amid the fears, a second sign with the same message as the first: Jesus was Lord.

I write this meditation during Holy Week, April 5–11, 2020. Likely some will remember this time as part of "Covid Spring." Global pandemic infection and fatality rates are soaring. The news today reported that a popular US high school teacher went from healthy and active to dead from the virus—in a week. I heard that and I mentally joined that crowd on the road to Jerusalem: I was scared.

But I needn't have been. You either. We can recall Jesus' non-attention-getting Holy Week signs and lay hold of the ancient church's gospel and battle-cry: "Jesus is Lord." We must, of course, pray and be prudent. But we must remember that amid hovering danger and seemingly out-of-control circumstances, Christ has things in hand. He is Lord.

That truth is the treasure.

Twelve

Outside Eden, God Was on the Case

". . . people began to call upon the name of the Lord."
—Genesis 4:26b

Genesis 4 has the sobering honour of being the first chapter in the Bible about life outside the Garden of Eden. Given the train wreck of chapter three—Adam and Eve breaking covenant with God—we expect chapter four to be a survey of the wreckage. And yes, there was darkness there: history's first murder (Genesis 4:8), Cain's refusal to trust God (Genesis 4:13), and the ominous beginnings of the anti-God city of man (Cain's city in 4:17, anticipating Babel). We're clearly not in Eden anymore.

But the text of chapter four doesn't allow the darkness centre stage. This was God's story. The chapter provides another example of bookending: beginning and ending a passage with the same idea, the writer's way of cluing us in to the intended point of the text.

Note the way the first chapter in the Bible's post-Eden history begins and ends. It begins with Eve seeing God at work in the birth of her first son: *"I have gotten a man with the help of the Lord"* (v. 1). That was the opening bookend. The Bible's post-fall world began with a testimony to the goodness of God. Outside Eden, the God of Eden was there. Eve realized it and testified to it.

Twenty-three verses later, we see the concluding bookend. Amid the lingering impact of the chapter three train wreck, God kept doing his faithfully faithful thing:

> *And Adam knew his wife again, and she bore a son and called his name Seth, for she said, "God has appointed for me another offspring instead of Abel, for Cain killed him." . . . At that time people began to call upon the name of the Lord.*
>
> —vv. 25, 26b

The birth of a child to a grieving woman, and history's very first prayer movement: In dark days outside of Eden, the God of Eden was on the case. His goodness outflanked humanity's sin—including mine and yours.

You may be in a Genesis 4 season. You may feel like Cain in Genesis 4:13b: it's *"more than I can bear"* (NIV). Those times come; however, if by faith we put our trust in Christ, he grafts our story into God's story. He will not leave us in Cain's city (Genesis 4:17); rather, he will make us to *be* a city—God's city, set on a hill (Psalm 48:1; Matthew 5:14)—with its own story. We have this treasure: in that story, God's goodness bookends all things.

Thirteen

How the Apostle Paul
Learned to Ride a Two-Wheeler

"O God, from my youth you have taught me ..."
—Psalm 71:17a

When my computer goes on the fritz, I phone my friend Christopher—a professional "I.T. guy." He does in minutes what I would need hours (if not days) to do. Why? Because he knows how. He has tech know-how.

This morning I was surprised to find a reference to "know-how" in Scripture. The apostle Paul wrote, *"I know how to be brought low, and I know how to abound. In any and every circumstance, I have learned the secret of facing plenty and hunger, abundance and need"* (Philippians 4:12). Paul, of course, wasn't talking about tech know-how. He was talking about *life* know-how—about how to navigate life. And he said he knew how to be brought low and how to abound. He knew how to face *"hunger and thirst* [and be] *poorly dressed ... buffeted and homeless"* (1 Corinthians 4:11). And he knew how to receive *"full payment, and more... [*and be*] well supplied"* (Philippians 4:18). How did he know how? He had learned how; he had *"learned the secret of facing plenty and hunger."*

Learning is usually done step by step: a child learning to ride a two-wheeler, or play the piano, or speak a second language, or swim. It takes patience and work. Paul (then Saul) learned in a sudden, blinding moment that Jesus of Nazareth was not (as he thought) a now-dead false prophet. He was the very-much-alive Lord of heaven (Acts 9:3–8). Paul learned this in his turning-point encounter on the road to Damascus. But he didn't learn "how to be brought low and how to abound" in a moment. That was like learning to ride a two-wheeler. It took time. And patience. And work.

Decades ago, Christian friends of mine—a husband and wife in full-time vocational ministry—watched helplessly as a financial scam vaporized their life savings. Poof. Gone. So what did they do? They learned. They learned know-how. Like a child learns to ride a two-wheeler bicycle, they learned. They learned to keep their eyes on God. They learned—patiently— to reset their goals: for their kids' education; for a nicer home; for their some-day, hoped-for comfortable retirement. They learned, through practice and patience, to turn away from self-pity ("Poor us!"), bitterness ("We'd like to get our hands on those people!") and regret ("We were fools!"). They learned how to downsize and how to rejoice in their downed size.

Today, some forty years later, they are faithfully and fruitfully serving God.

They never got the money back.

They're ok with that. The know-how was their treasure.

Fourteen

Why Your Efforts Are Not in Vain

"... yes, establish the work of our hands!"

—Psalm 90:17b

In the closing minutes of the movie version of *The Fellowship of the Ring* (part one of The Lord of the Rings series), the film's heroes face a hope-crushing defeat. They get trounced in battle and scattered from one another. Three of them—Gimli, Legolas, and Aragorn—regroup. They are weary and shaken. "So it has all been in vain!" laments Gimli. Gimli is the stalwart dwarf-warrior and one of the film's few sources of comic relief. But not now. Not here.

Lord of the Rings spoiler alert: In the end, the good guys win.

But Gimli's reaction is true to life. And Christians have their Gimli moments: in cancer wards, in divorce courts, in projects that bear no visible fruit. Gimli's lament reminds us of Ecclesiastes: *"Vanity of vanities ... All is vanity"* (1:2).

Is that true? It was certainly true in Ecclesiastes. This enigmatic book looked at life through the window of Genesis 3: thorns guaranteed (v. 18) and *"to dust you shall return"* (v. 19b). That was Genesis 3's lens on life—and Ecclesiastes adopted it.[11] So were the thorns the final word? Was Gimli right?

The apostle Paul had an answer. In 1 Corinthians 15:58, he said, *"Therefore ... be steadfast, immovable, always abounding in the work of the Lord, knowing that in the Lord your labor is not in vain."* (Note those last three words!) That impacting promise was part of a new window. Ecclesiastes' window was Adam bringing death (Ecclesiastes 7:29. 8:8). Paul's window was Christ bringing life: restored bodies on the Last Day (1 Corinthians 15) and restored knowledge of God now (the treasure!).

In the meantime, in our trounced-and-scattered moments, how do we hold on to the *"not in vain"* promise? By heeding what the promise says: *"in the Lord your labor is not in vain."* Note those words, *"in the Lord."* Our labour is, like us, "in Christ."

Think back to Christ lifting a sinking Peter out of the stormy sea and setting him into the boat (Matthew 14:31-32). Even so, God has lifted us out of Adam and set us into Christ: *"And because of him* [God] *you are in Christ Jesus"* (1 Corinthians 1:30a, see also 15:47–49; Romans 5:13–21). In themselves, our works are limited, flawed, and prone to setbacks. But God has taken us up into Christ—and our works as well: "... *in the Lord your labor is not in vain.*" That hope is the new window. It's part of the treasure.

Are our works setback-prone? Definitely. In vain? Definitely not. They are "*in the Lord,*" and—setbacks notwithstanding—God will work through them. Good and significant things will happen. And spoiler alert: the good guys are going to win.

Fifteen

Had His Batteries Run Low?

"Having eyes do you not see . . . ?"

—Mark 8:18a

Mark 8:22–26 recounts Jesus granting sight to a blind man. But the scene is about more than yet-one-more miracle in an already miracle-rich ministry. Mark employs it to say something about what it meant to believe in Christ—that is, to "see." Notice three things about this miraculous restoration of sight.

First, the timing: The healing took place right before the hinge-moment of the whole book, when Peter "saw" that Jesus was the Christ (8:29). Mark played out the blind man seeing as the lead-up to Peter seeing.

Second, the bond Jesus established with the man: *"And he took the blind man by the hand and led him out of the village"* (8:23a). Likely, the blind man had no idea where he was. What did he have to hold on to? Christ's hand. Nothing else. All other supports were gone. Then Jesus spat into the man's blind eyes.

Side bar: How close are we prepared for Jesus to get to us? Do we trust him enough to risk feeling awkward? Embarrassed?

Third, the puzzle: It took Jesus two touches to restore the blind man's sight. After one touch, the man saw, but only partly: *"I see people, but they look like trees, walking"* (8:24b). After a second shot, the man *"saw everything clearly"* (8:25b).

Hello? Jesus calmed a storm with a word and raised Jairus's daughter from death—and he couldn't fix blindness without a second hit? Had his batteries run low? No. In Mark's telling, the two-step healing is about what it meant to believe. The passage highlights the disciples' slow and partial "seeing." In the very next scene, Peter declared *"You are the Christ"* (8:29b), only to then rebuke Jesus for committing to the way of the cross (8:32)!

Peter saw but didn't see. He declared Jesus to be the Christ, but he didn't like this talk about suffering and death (8:31). Peter's grasp of the gospel was like the blind man's sight after Jesus' first touch: hazy and partial. Later events—the transfiguration, the resurrection, and the day of Pentecost—would give Peter his second touch. He would go on to declare Jesus' whole story—both the miracles and the suffering—as God's plan (Acts 2:22–23, 10:38–39).

The church today is full of first-touch-only Simons: people with a hazy gospel. Much of the time, I'm one of them.

Come, Lord Jesus. Grip our hands. Lead us out of our villages.

Embarrass us. (Go ahead, spit.)

Touch us again. Be our treasure.

Sixteen

If "All Things Hold Together," What About That Ship?

"... upholding all things by the word of his power ..."
—Hebrews 1:3, KJV

" ♦ ♦ ♦ **[** *H*^e^ *is before all things,"* wrote Paul, *"and in him all things hold together"* (Colossians 1:17). Depending on who is translating, that verse might read "in him all things continue." The "him," of course, is Christ. In him everything continues. It holds together.

Ponder this: These words came to us from a man who a couple years earlier watched the ship he was sailing in run aground in a storm and break apart in the surf (Acts 27:41). The passengers survived, but the vessel disintegrated. *"All things hold together"*? What about that ship? And what about Paul's ministry partnership with Barnabas—the one that so famously busted up (Acts 15:39)? Or that church plant you joined (the one that went to pieces)? Or your cousin's six-month marriage? Paul's *"all things hold together"* statement sounds very grand. But does it account for how messy life is?

Paul knew all about messy. His Acts 27 shipwreck wasn't his only "things go to pieces" moment. Second Corinthians 11:24–29 provides a partial inventory of his suffering as an apostle (reader discretion advised). And later, near the end of his life, he faced "great harm" from enemies and abandonment by friends (2 Timothy 4:14–18). But Paul believed in a Creator King whose plan and command fenced in all things and all outcomes. God said to the bursting-forth primeval seas, *"Thus far shall you come, and no farther"* (Job 38:11a). After the Genesis flood, he mercifully preserved the world through the stability of regular seasons (Genesis 8:22) and social order (Genesis 9:6). All this was part of all things holding together. Paul knew that God, in Christ, had all things in hand—primeval seas, Mediterranean northeasters, shipwrecks, and Barnabas bust-ups included. The hold-all-things-together lordship of Jesus didn't remove traumatic events; rather, like a harbour with its water, it surrounded them.

And speaking of storms, the sea was unruly, but God ruled it: *"The Lord sits enthroned over the flood"* (Psalm 29:10a). Sometimes he ruled it by restraining it (*"Thus far … and no farther"*). Sometimes he ruled it by rebuking it (*"Peace! Be still!"* Mark 4:39; also Psalm 106:9). And sometimes he ruled it by recruiting it. Job said to God: *"… you toss me about in the roar of the storm"* (Job 30:22b). But later, he said, *"I had heard of you by the hearing of the ear, but now my eye sees you"* (42:5). God had recruited the storm to do a work in Job. Job came out changed, in what one commentator called an "enlarged life with God."[12] God restraining, rebuking, recruiting things and outcomes: in Christ, all things hold together. Result? People—Job and others like him—with a bigger treasure.

May you and I join them. Your cousin, too.

Seventeen

The God Who
Threaded the Needle

"With God are wisdom and might . . ."

—Job 12:13a

The book of Romans ends with one of Paul's famously rich doxologies: *"Now to him who is able to strengthen you . . . to the only wise God be glory forevermore"* (16:25–27). Doxologies are praise-texts, and Romans 16:25–27 isn't the only doxology in Romans. There's another one in 11:33, 36b: *"Oh, the depth of the . . . wisdom . . . of God . . . To him be glory forever."* Both doxologies praise God for the same thing: his wisdom.

Romans was Paul's answer to a raft of issues: how we are set right with God (by faith, not works), how we live for God (by the Spirit, not by the law), how God incorporates Gentiles and Jews into a single family, with joint-access to him, and how Jewish believers who still observed Old Testament festivals could live in unity with Gentile believers, who didn't know

Passover from a screwdriver. All these themes had to do with being right with God and living right for God.

When it's time for the closing doxology, then, we expect something like, "Now to him who justifies us through Jesus." But what we get is Paul exalting God as *"the only wise God."* So why conclude a letter about justification, faith, and unity with a doxology about God being wise? Well, think back. The entire book of Romans—indeed, the entire Bible—testifies to God's wisdom. Here was a God who, in the face of tangled, sometimes painful, circumstances, knew what to do. Over and again, his wisdom was deep. He threaded the needle. He solved the problem.

A fallen humanity? The "only wise God" made a way. Amid the guilty descendants of Adam, God raised up a new father-of-a-people: Abraham (Genesis 12-17; Romans 4). He declared Abraham righteous on the basis of his faith, and he does the same for his believing descendants (Romans 4:23–24). Fallen humanity? The wise God came up with a plan: he founded a new humanity. He threaded the needle.

A tension between God's justice and his mercy (as in Hosea 11:8)? The "only wise God" made a way: He sent Christ *"as a propitiation by his blood . . . so that he might be just and the justifier of the one who has faith in Jesus"* (Romans 3:25-26) (Note that all-important "and"!). Justice and mercy fulfilled. Eye of the needle, thread in the hand of God. Done. God's wisdom is deep.

49

You may face your own tangle: sickness that stays, marriage tensions you thought Christians didn't have, home-schooled Christian kids who are worse behaved than the grade-school pagans across the street. Whatever the issue, and however painful, remember: God knows how to thread the needle. Being assured of that is finding the treasure.

Eighteen

The "Why Cry" Was a Signal

"So Jesus also suffered outside the gate ..."

—Hebrews 13:12a

When Christ cried out on the cross, *"My God, my God, why have you forsaken me?"* (Mark 15:34b), what was going on? Did Jesus die bewildered? How do we read this moment?

We read it by attending to Jesus' actual words. They weren't random—they were Scripture, specifically the opening line of Psalm 22. This psalm is a classic, three-stage Hebrew lament: anguish, heart-turn, and hope:

- Anguish: *"... why...?"* (v. I)
- Heart-turn: *"But you ... O my help ..."* (vv. I9, 20)
- Hope: *"All the ends of the earth shall remember and turn to the Lord"* (v. 27a)[13]

Psalm 22 stands beneath a heading: "To the choirmaster: according to The Doe of the Dawn. A Psalm of David." The point? Israel adopted David's anguish-born song as part of their corporate worship ("To the choirmaster"). The assigned melody ("Doe of the Dawn") pointed to in-breaking light—that is, to hope.[14] And verse twenty-seven promised a world worshipping God. Neither in its birth in David's tumultuous life nor in its deployment in Israel's worship was this psalm about bewilderment. It was a song about hope: doe of the *dawn*.

How do we read the why-cry when Jesus is on the cross? Was he simply voicing the anguish of verse one? Or signaling the "dawn" message of the whole psalm? It was the latter. Jesus always saw his suffering as part of God's plan: The Son of Man must suffer—and rise again (Mark 8:31, 9:31, 10:34). "... [*Let*] *the Scriptures be fulfilled*," he said at his arrest (Mark 14:49). He would be the ultimate Passover lamb: "*This is my blood of the covenant*" (Mark 14:24a). The woman's perfume-offering the night before he died would be—he said—an anointing for his "burial," and anointing always spoke of purpose. Both his death and her offering would be "*proclaimed in the whole world*" (Mark 14:9). Yet again, a vision for "all the ends of the earth."

Jesus did not die bewildered.

So why the *why*? Because that was how Psalm 22 began – and Psalm 22 began with anguish but ended with hope. Jesus was sending a signal—a signal that even as he entered our separation from God ("Why have you forsaken me?") he was holding *on* to God: "*My God, my God.*" And a signal that he was God's wrap-up not just to Psalm 22's opening line but to the entire psalm: anguish, heart-turn, hope. His death would bring a dawn: "*All the ends of the earth shall remember and turn to the Lord*" (Psalm 22:27a).[15]

Behold! I tell you a mystery: cut off from God *with* us, Jesus held on to God *for* us. He is our dawn. And he is our treasure.

Nineteen

Earth's Dust, God's Breath

". . . he breathed on them . . ."

—John 20:22

Scripture says God made the first man using a grand total of two ingredients: *"then the Lord God formed a man from the dust of the ground and breathed into his nostrils the breath of life"* (Genesis 2:7a). Dust and God's own breath. That was it.

Dust was lifeless. To die was to return to dust (Genesis 3:19). Dust was a small step above nothing. But Adam and his dust-people descendants did some remarkable things. They caught fish (1:26), filled and subdued the earth (1:28), dug for gold (2:12), practised agriculture (2:15), made up names for animals (2:19), spoke in verse (2:23), joined in marriage (2:24), had kids (4:1), and raised livestock (4:20). They invented things: the banjo and the clarinet (4:21) and tents and tractors (4:22).

And chess. And penicillin. And microchips.

And they wrote things, like Psalm 19 (give it a read!). C.S. Lewis called it "one of the greatest lyrics in the world."[16] And like Gerard Manley Hopkins' poem "God's Grandeur," the closing lines of which picture God's Spirit giving hope to a sin-damaged creation: "Because the Holy Ghost over the bent/World broods with warm breast and with ah! bright wings."[17] And like Mark's Gospel, which bookended the Jesus story with a torn sky (1:10) and a torn curtain (15:38). Two tearings, both pointing to Christ, the mender of the world.[18]

And they built things, like cities with towers (2 Samuel 5:9; Psalm 48), and a temple for God to dwell in (1 Kings 5. And note verse six—the nations helped!). And they studied botany and zoology (1 Kings 4:33). And raised kids (Deuteronomy 31:12–13). And made wine (Psalm 104:15). And designed, built, and sailed ships (Psalm 104:26).

And long after Eden, by God's unbelief-reversing grace, they started history's first prayer movement (Genesis 4:26). And—much later—they took the gospel of Christ *"from Jerusalem and all the way around to Illyricum"* (Romans 15:19). And Canada. And Irian Jaya. And—even as I write this—are rescuing children from sex and labour slavery on six continents. They're called the International Justice Mission.[19]

Quite a resumé for creatures made of dust. It must have been the breath.

And note Christ's triumphant missional climax to this story: He rose again and did a replay of Genesis 2:7: "... *he breathed on them and said to them, 'Receive the Holy Spirit'"* (John 20:22). The story began with the breath. And in Jesus it began again.

So go, dust-people: invent, write, build, sail, make wine, raise kids, and carry the gospel. The breath is on you. And the Giver of that breath is your treasure.

Twenty

Galactic Comfort

"For as high as the heavens ... so great is his steadfast love ..."
—Psalm 103:11

The last four Christmases, I've given myself the same present: calendars featuring full-colour, 12" x 12 ½" photos of galaxies. Most are from the Hubble telescope. The image on the wall as I type shows a nebula: a luminous, sapphire-blue cosmic cloud, the footprint of an exploded star. The image is 12" x 12 ½". The nebula itself, astronomers tell us, is five-and-a-half light years across. That's 32 trillion miles. (Yes, *trillion.*) The images in these calendars always comfort me. They point me to God.

Comfort through glory: This is the theme of one of Scripture's stand-out chapters, Isaiah 40. This passage is a hymn to God's greatness—shown in saving his people (vv. 1–11) and in ruling his world, distant stars included (vv.

12–31). It begins with the words *"Comfort, comfort my people"* (v. 1) and goes on to catalogue the ways God is great (note the link between comfort and greatness).

This great God rules the stars the way a shepherd leads his sheep: *"He ... calls forth each of them by name ... not one of them is missing"* (v. 26, NIV). It's a picture from the created order (the stars) of the way God works with his people. So when that image looks out at me from my office wall and says, "Your God made me. He's that big," I feel comforted.

In verse twenty-seven, Isaiah addressed the complaint of the people, who felt ignored by God: *"Why do you say ... 'my right is disregarded by my God'?"* There is rebuke here: *"Why do you say?"* But there is comfort too. Isaiah went on: *"The Lord is the everlasting God, the Creator of the ends of the earth. He does not faint or grow weary; his understanding is unsearchable"* (v. 28).

Here is the comfort: God has no limits. He is not limited by time: he is *"the everlasting God."* He is not limited by distance: he is *"the Creator of the ends of the earth."* He is not limited in strength: *"He does not faint or grow weary."* And he is not limited in wisdom: *"His understanding is unsearchable."* When we're in a "Lord, what's going on?" season, we need to know his wisdom is greater than ours. And it is. It's unsearchable.

I finish writing this at 11:00 p.m. Today wasn't an easy day, but Isaiah said God calls me the way he calls on individual stars: *"by name."* Knowing I am known by a no-limits God:

that's the treasure. I ponder the photo on the wall. I feel more ready for tomorrow.

Comforted, even.

Twenty-One

The Coming of the Spirit Was an Act of War

"He parted the heavens and came down"

—Psalm 18:9a, NIV

Rival street gangs often stake claim to a territory, or "turf": "What're you doing here, punk? This is *our* turf!" In gang culture, the wrong place can be a dark place—a place where your enemy is in control.

There are dark places, and there are dark seasons: "Since the gangs came in, it's been very dark. This last year has belonged to them." Time itself can become the enemy's turf. Ask people in conflict-zones: "I don't think I've heard people laugh since the Boko Haram came." Ask children whose daddy has been sent to prison: "It's sad at our house now."

So whose turf is history? I mean, world history, church history, your family's history? Bible history (Eden to New Jerusalem)? Your own history? Whose turf is it? God's, of course: *"from everlasting to everlasting, you are God"* (Psalm 90:2b). *"My times are in your hands"* (Psalm 31:15a). God said, *"I make known the end from the beginning, from ancient times, what is still to come"* (Isaiah 46:10a, NIV).

Time is God's turf. Or is it? Didn't Paul call the time we're in *"the present evil age"* (Galatians 1:4)? Didn't he call Satan *"the god of this age"* (2 Corinthians 4:4, NIV)? Can we really call it "God's turf"?

We can, and Scripture gives us the reason. On the Day of Pentecost, Peter preached to the crowds about the ascension of Christ and the descent of the Spirit (Acts 2). He spoke about *"blood, fire and billows of smoke"* (Acts 2:19, quoting Joel 2:30, NIV). Blood, fire, and smoke: battlefield images. Why? Because the coming of the Holy Spirit was an act of war: God was invading the present evil age. Pentecost was about God himself showing up. His mighty wind-and-flame arrival said, "Satan's turf? We'll see about that."

A generation later, Paul wrote these words: *"To the King of the ages, immortal, invisible, the only God, be honor and glory forever and ever. Amen"* (1 Timothy 1:17). High octane stuff. You could do your devotions for a week just pondering that verse. And don't miss that lead-off phrase, *"the King of the ages."* The ages? What ages? *All* the ages—*"the present evil age"* included.

If your life at the moment is a battlefield (emotional, moral, relational, financial), then remember this: The present evil age belongs to the King of the ages. By sending his Spirit, he was showing himself to be King and claiming for himself the time and place where you stand.

No need to fear the street thugs. Your life is God's turf. Knowing that is the treasure.

Twenty-Two

How to Tilt Your Cosmos
(Or, Passion for the One Thing)

"But one thing I do ..."

—Philippians 3:13

We all know a version of the story. Here's the way I heard it: A ninety-five-pound woman lifted a two-thousand-pound car off her teenage son. The jack had slipped, and Eddie was pinned underneath. Spontaneously, unthinkingly, Mom reached beneath the vehicle and bare-handedly lifted it off him. She screamed to his little sister, "Pull him out!" Ten-year-old Lucy pulled seventeen-year-old Eddie to safety. Mom dropped the car onto the pavement. Bang!

Ninety-five versus two thousand, and the ninety-five won.

What happened? In that sickening, slipped-jack, metal-on-bone moment, that woman's worldview changed. Her cosmos tilted. Life suddenly got very, very uncomplicated: *save* him. Just that. Just one thing. Every "What about my back?"

thought vaporized. In her newly tilted cosmos, her back didn't matter. All that mattered was one thing.

Ditto, Christians. God calls us to live for one thing: the glory of Christ. We join a rescue op (like Eddie from beneath the car) that is also an announcement op: declaring Christ's rescue of *us*. Knowing him and making him known. For Christians, exalting Christ is the "one thing" (Psalm 27:4; Luke 10:42).

Paul wrote his letter to the Philippians during a two-year time of house-arrest (Acts 28:30–31; Philippians 1:7,13,14,17). He lacked any outward, earthly guarantee that his imprisonment wouldn't end in death. In those days, he became that woman by the road: only one thing mattered. For Paul, it was glorifying Christ: "... *it is my eager expectation and hope that I will not be at all ashamed, but that with full courage now as always Christ will be honored in my body, whether by life or by death*" (Philippians 1:20). His own outcomes didn't matter. Christ's glory mattered. That was Paul's one thing.

Do our outcomes matter? ("Lord, help me land that job!"). Yes—but they don't stand at the front of the line. They stand in line behind the one thing. And if we let God tilt our cosmos, we'll be ok with that: "*For the sake of Christ, then, I am content with weaknesses, insults, hardships, persecutions, and calamities*" (2 Corinthians 12:10a).

That's how to tilt your cosmos: Realize that your life—like Paul's—is *"for the sake of Christ."* He is our treasure. All other things we fret about get knocked out of the centre.

Welcome to a less complicated way to live.

A ninety-five-pound local church—with a passion for the one thing—versus a two-thousand-pound obstacle.

Guess who wins.

Twenty-Three

Feeling Lost Doesn't Mean You Are

"These forty years the Lord your God has been with you ..."
—Deuteronomy 2:7b

"Not all those who wander are lost"—hope-restoring words from J.R.R. Tolkien, and one of the reasons I love *The Lord of the Rings*. They come from a poem, and they refer to Aragorn, one of the story's heroes. The poem reads (in part):

All that is gold does not glitter,
Not all those who wander are lost;
The old that is strong does not wither,
Deep roots are not reached by the frost.[20]

Aragorn's life was a wanderer's life. For obscure decades, he lived as an itinerant guardian of vulnerable, isolated communities in Middle-Earth (hapless hobbit villages among them). To many, he was unremarkable. People eyed him with suspicion, mocking his never-settle-down life. But he was more than he seemed: beneath his weather-beaten exterior lay hope for all of Middle Earth. (Read the book—you'll see why.)

I first read the "Not all those who wander are lost" poem some forty years ago. I still love and savour it. When I feel directionless, the words remind me of Aragorn. They kindle confidence about facing the future.

This hope-restoring vision, of course, is way older than *The Lord of the Rings*. It goes clear back to Deuteronomy, where God gave Israel the original not-all-those-who-wander-are-lost window on life. In their worship of God, Israel was to confess, "*A wandering Aramean was my father*" (Deuteronomy 26:5a). The words referred to their ancestor, Jacob. Jacob's life was a wanderer's life. His wandering was a consequence of cheating his brother, Esau, out of his birthright (Genesis 27–28). Esau vowed revenge, and Jacob fled north to Aram ("Padan-Aram" in Genesis 28) and a decades-long exile. Hence the phrase, "wandering Aramean." Israel's corporate wandering (their forty years in the wilderness) echoed the Jacob story. Jacob wandered, and so did his descendants (Deuteronomy 8:2, 29:5).

It was near the end of that forty-year wandering that God told them to employ the "wandering Aramean" refrain in their worship. The words said, in effect, "Like our wandering father

Jacob, we are a wandering people. Because we are wanderers, we need God to look after us. And he does. So we worship him." Recalling Jacob's wandering helped Israel embrace their own. And it magnified God's mercy.

Wanderers, yes. Lost, no. Jacob's God was their God. And ours. Not all those who wander are lost. Offered up to God, even our self-caused delays and directionless days can glorify him.

Which means that even when we feel like we're lost, we're not.

Twenty-Four

Why Mopping Floors
Is Wearing a Crown

". . . the earth he has given to the children of man."

—Psalm 115:16

Genesis 1 isn't the Bible's only teaching on God creating the world. Other texts weigh in as well. Some highlight the creation events themselves (Job 38:1–11). Others focus on how the created order fits together (Psalm 104, 115:16; Colossians 1:16–17), or how it testified to God's greatness (Psalm 19:1; Revelation 5:13).

Among the how-it-fit-together passages is David's prayer in Psalm 8:5–6: "[You] *have ... crowned him* [humanity] *with glory ... You have given him dominion over the works of your hands..."* David, of course, was recalling Genesis 1:26 (*"Let them have dominion"*) about humanity's role in God ruling. God rules through people. David saw honour and dignity here: to exercise dominion is to wear a crown. And wearing this crown (as we see in Genesis 1–2) meant being fruitful and multiplying, filling and subduing the earth, and caring for the garden. In Psalm 104, it meant routine work: *"Man goes out to his work and to his labor until the evening. O Lord, how manifold are your works!"* (vv. 23–24a). Note the link between those two statements: Humanity's daily work is part of God's "works."

Park those thoughts and ponder these from G.E. Veith in *God at Work*:

> When we pray the Lord's Prayer ... we ask God to give us this day our daily bread. And He does give us our daily bread. He does it by means of the farmer who planted and harvested the grain, the baker who made the flour into bread, the person who prepared our meal. We might today add the truck drivers who hauled the produce, the factory workers in the food processing plant, the warehouse men, the wholesale distributors, the stock boys, the lady at the checkout counter. Also playing their part are the bankers, futures investors, advertisers, lawyers, agricultural scientists, mechanical engineers, and every other player in the nation's economic system. All of these were instrumental in enabling you to eat your morning bagel.[21]

When I was an undergraduate college student, I used to join in on late-night, sometimes pretentious, dorm sessions on the meaning of life. Some of my dorm-mates said there was none. I was a new Christian, convinced there was, but struggling to articulate it—even to myself. And what about routine, not-very-glamorous work, like mopping warehouse floors? Does that have "meaning"?

Indeed it does. When we cultivate fields, mop floors, shovel snow (I live in Winnipeg!), wash dishes, or care for kids, we are working. And our working is part of God ruling. Does it have meaning? Of course. It's part of wearing the crown. And part of the treasure.

Twenty-Five

Fully Man, Fully God

"Isaiah ... saw [Christ's] glory and spoke of him."

—John 12:41

Centuries before Christ appeared on earth, he appeared in the book of Isaiah. The prophet credited him with remarkable things: rescuing God's people from gloom (9:1), caring for the bruised reed (42:3), winning forgiveness for our sins (52:13–53:12), and working in the bruised reeds to make them into sturdy oaks (61:3), forgiven and strong. How would Christ do these remarkable things? Because he would be fully man and fully God.

Consider: Isaiah based his rescue-from-gloom promise (9:1–6) squarely on Christ's humanity and deity: *"... there will be no gloom ... For to us a child is born ... and his name shall be called ... Mighty God."* Note: a *child* who would be *born.* That is, fully human.[22] But astoundingly—in the very same verse— *"his name shall be called ... Mighty God."* Fully human, but also fully God.

Fully human? Yes. So human he would walk through that heart-cloud we all know: "What's the use?" Christ would face it and say so: *"But my work seems so useless! I have spent my strength for nothing and to no purpose"* (Isaiah 49:4a, NLT).[23] That weary weight of pointlessness. But this weary man would be a faithful man. In the face of futility (Matthew 17:17; 26:40), he stayed with the script: *"Yet I leave it all in the Lord's hand; I will trust God for my reward"* (Isaiah 49:4b NLT). One of us. But faithful.

Fully God? Yes. Isaiah called him "Mighty God"—a title (in the very next chapter) for God himself (10:21). And "mighty" like David's "mighty men" (2 Samuel 23:16—the same word in Hebrew). Men who did exploits against Philistine armies. Christ would do exploits too, against another kind of army. (Ask Legion!)

Fully human? Yes. Human enough to draw alongside emotionally damaged, *"bruised reed"* people (Isaiah 42:3)—like the disheartened disciples on the Emmaus Road. He *"opened to* [them] *the Scriptures"* so their hearts burned (Luke 24:32). Bruised reeds on the way to being mighty oaks (Isaiah 61:3).

Fully God? Yes. Christ is the only person in Scripture to share the description "high and lifted up" with Yahweh himself. In Isaiah 6:1 and 57:15, the prophet used this exalted phrase for Yahweh, the eternal covenant God. But in 52:13, he applied it to Jesus.

There are imponderables here: How did the God who never became weary (Psalm 121:4; Isaiah 40:28) become a man who did (Isaiah 49:4a; John 4:6) and yet remain God (John 20:28)? Behold, one of the "hidden things" Moses told Israel to expect (Deuteronomy 29:29). Best to leave it hidden and rejoice. Christ was fully man and fully God. Whatever we're facing, he is our enabling. And our treasure.

Twenty-Six

Roosters on Steeples: Why They're Good News

"...sinners, of whom I am the foremost."

—I Timothy I:15b

Historians of architecture say no one knows for sure who first came up with the "rooster on the rooftop" idea. We see them—metal silhouettes of chickens—on housetops, barn-roofs, and church steeples. There are tentative theories about how this tradition started. Here's one that makes sense to me, especially with the steeples.

The rooster-image recalled that the Christian faith was born, in part, in a failure-story: Simon Peter's three-fold denial of Christ, heralded by the rooster's crow (Mark 14:30, 53–72). Peter had been bravado-man: *"Even though they all fall away, I will not"* (Mark 14:29). But Jesus gave him an ego-deflating warning: *"... this very night, before the rooster crows twice, you will deny me three times"* (Mark 14:30b). Which was, of course, exactly what Peter did. And on denial number three, the rooster crowed. Mark's account opens up the depths beneath this scene by showing that Simon's lying took place at the same time as Jesus' truth-speaking.[24] Darkness and light, side by side.

While Peter was denying Jesus to a servant girl and her friends (who had zero authority), Jesus was declaring himself to be God's Son to the high priest (who had formidable power). Peter saved his own skin. Jesus signed his own death warrant. Then the rooster crowed. Light dawned on Jesus' crucifixion day, and truth dawned in Peter's conflicted mind. He saw what he had done. Shame avalanched down on him: *"And he went out and wept bitterly"* (Matthew 26:75b).

But Simon's story was not over.

Remember the angel's words to the women at the empty tomb: *"He has risen ... But go, tell his disciples and Peter that he is going before you to Galilee"* (Mark 16:6b–7a). Note who alone among the disciples came in for personal mention: rooster man. The Lord still wanted Simon on the team. Through Christ, the denier of Christ had a future in Christ. He would be included in the pre-Pentecost discipling trip to Galilee.[25] At Pentecost, he would boldly declare the gospel in Jerusalem (Acts 2). He would write two letters that would become part of the Bible. He would glorify God by dying for Christ (John 21:19).

Roosters on steeples? They are proclamations. In their quiet, undramatic way, they say, "Come, all who have failed

Christ—but whom Christ has not failed. He has risen and he calls you by name, and he goes before you." Where? Initially to Galilee—where it all began. For Simon Peter, it was about to begin again.

I for one am glad of the rooster custom. Beneath that sign is hope and welcome—and a future.

Twenty-Seven

Swimming Upstream (Part One)

"But you, O Lord, are ... the lifter of my head."

—Psalm 3:3

Two days past Christmas I suffered a heart attack. It landed me in hospital for four nights, where my doctors ran endless tests, installed a stent, and sent me home with a bag of meds and a list of things I'm not allowed to do: can't drive a car, can't lift anything weighing more than three pounds, can't climb stairs more than three times a day. The meds keep the fibrillations away, but they keep my energy away too. So I take two naps a day and depend on Velma. I know I'll get through it. Still, mentally and physically, the situation is draining. I often feel like those much-photographed salmon in British Columbia waterfalls: swimming upstream.

I've been thinking of faithful people who swam upstream—and how they did it. Saint Paul was one. He discovered a response to life that enabled him to swim against the current. It kept him moving forward in the face of weaknesses, insults, hardships, persecutions, and calamities. That enabling response was contentment. He chose to be content. And contentment kept him swimming upstream.

Contentment is a choice. It reminds itself that Jesus isn't just Lord of the loaves and fish. He is Lord of the loaves and fish *"in the desolate place"* (Mark 6:31). He's able to look after his people *there*. Recall Paul's inventory of opposing currents in 2 Corinthians 12:10: *"For the sake of Christ, then, I am content with weaknesses, insults, hardships, persecutions, and calamities. For when I am weak, then I am strong."*

Weaknesses? Paul wasn't first for this one. Jacob limped (Genesis 32:31). Moses was a poor public speaker (Exodus 4:10). And Paul had health issues that affected his ministry-travel and were a trial to his hosts (Galatians 4:13–14). If we believe his words in 2 Corinthians 12:10, we will see that he trusted in Christ in the face of all these and chose contentment in the midst of his weakness. And kept swimming.

Insults? Mercifully, I've been spared this one on this recent adventure. But insults have a cousin: irritations. As in nurse at 3:00 a.m. "Mr. Perry, I need you to take this pill." So, once again, pastor Paul. What would this contentment-choosing, upstream swimmer have told me? Probably, "Stop feeling sorry for yourself! Take the pill and bless the nurse. She's part of Christ looking after you in the desolate place. Be content!"

Twenty-Eight

Swimming Upstream (Part Two)

Hardships? In terms of scale, mine are dust next to Paul's. Recall his two-week storm at sea experience in Acts 27. Fourteen straight days of howling winds and ship-battering seas. The crew went days without food. Paul? He showed heroic pastoral care for his 276 shipmates. He urged them to eat. He gave wise counsel to the captain. When the ship ran aground, he joined in gathering wood for a fire to stave off the cold. He shook off a viper—and self-pity with it. And he stood gratefully near the warmth of the flames, uncomplaining, content that "Christ is able to look after me *here*."

Persecutions? I recall another hospital visit, many years ago—not to recover from an illness but to picket on the sidewalk for the rights of unborn children. Again and again, a vanload of loud critics drove by. Back and forth they went, shouting obscenities at our demonstration. Emotionally, that got to me more than it should have. So what would upstream-apostle

Paul have done? He would have set his face into the oncoming current and blessed it as it hit him. And been content. And kept swimming.

Calamities? That's what my heart attack was. Family gathered for a Christmas season meal at a nice restaurant. Just finishing. Lots of good vibes and laughter around the table. *Crème brûlées* arrive (aaahhhh). I feel content. But a contentment test is about to strike. Chest pains, heart-thumping, choking sensation, stiff left arm, dizziness, clamminess of face and hands. All signs my wife (a former nurse) instantly recognized.

In minutes, we're in the emergency ward: blood-pressure cuffs, IV drips, and endless questions from the nurses. An ironic moment when the electric paddles twice fail to stop the fibrillation, and the doctor resorts to injections. He comments, "Mr. Perry, you have a stubborn heart." (If only he knew!) Then four nights of tubes, wires, monitors, tests and more tests, through-the-night PA announcements ("Dr. Whitley, call 378"), pill-taking, and blood-drawing. And electrodes stuck to my chest, checking to make sure I hadn't checked out. But closer than those electrodes, the promise of God: that Christ is able to care for me in the midst of the wires and the tubes. And the Spirit's call to be content with that—the choice that enables us to keep swimming upstream.

Twenty-Nine

From His Fullness
We Have All Received

". . . whoever comes to me shall not hunger . . ."

—John 6:35

One upside of having a heart attack—as I did a few weeks before writing this—is learning to live with lack: lack of energy, lack of concentration, lack of emotional stamina. If you're a Christian, lack has an upside: it pushes you into Christ, in whom there is no lack. As John said in the prologue to his Gospel, *"For from his fullness we have all received, grace upon grace"* (John 1:16). Eleven words that shape the whole book. And can shape our whole life.

The idea of fullness "bookends" John's story. Beginning and end, Jesus met people in their lack and showed his abundance. A wedding where the wine had run out (2:1-12): that was lack. Then, suddenly, six large jars of water (*"each holding twenty or thirty gallons,"* v. 6) brimming with top-quality wine (vv. 9-10)!

That was fullness. In the face of lack—no wine left—that was abundance. Our lack (Ever felt empty?), and "his fullness." The story had begun.

That was the front bookend. Now notice the concluding one: The risen Christ met his weary, up-all-night disciples. Up all night in a boat on the sea, fishing, and all they had to show for it was empty nets (21:1–14). That was lack.

Suddenly, a stranger on the beach (who wasn't really a stranger), called out, *"'Cast the net on the right side of the boat.' So, they cast it, and were not able to haul it in, because of the quantity of fish"* (v. 6). John reported seven men in that boat (v. 2). Fourteen arms couldn't pull in that catch. Soon enough, they (sore arms and all) sat down on the beach for a fish breakfast with the risen Jesus as their host (v. 12). That was fullness.

Jesus taught that the Last Day will come, when he will raise us up in new bodies (John 6:40). Then there will be no lack. That day is coming. It hasn't come yet. People still get heart attacks, face physical and emotional lack, run out of wine, and take their boats out fishing and come home empty. John knew all that when he sat down to write the first chapter of his Gospel. He knew his readers lived in lack-world. Still, he unfurled the abundance banner over the story to come: *"For from his fullness, we have all received, grace upon grace."* Good news, now.

We live in a yet-to-be-renewed world. But in its yet-to-be-renewed state, Jesus is Lord of wine and fish. Our lack is real, but it is not the last word. His fullness is. And that's the treasure.

Thirty

Let Your "What Ifs?" Become "Even Ifs!"

"Jacob ... poured out a drink offering ..."

—Genesis 35:14

It's a fear that visits me often—sometimes at three or four in the morning: "What if?" What if Jeff doesn't get that job? What if the house doesn't sell? What if I commit to that preaching invitation and flub it?

The apostle Paul had an answer for the "What if?" fear-trap. His answer to "What if?" was "Even if!" In Philippians 2:17, he said, *"Even if I am to be poured out as a drink offering upon the sacrificial offering of your faith, I am glad and rejoice with you all."* His point: If his current imprisonment ended in a death-sentence, he was ok with that. He wasn't clinging to his life, to his ministry, to a particular I'm-banking-on-it outcome, or anything else. He was clinging to God (Deuteronomy 10:20), which meant he could let go of everything else. *"Even if I am to be poured out . . ."*—that is, even if Rome puts me to death for the sake of Christ—*"I am glad."* His treasure was Christ.

Paul's letter to the Philippians spoke well of the church there. They were big-hearted people and generous in their financial support of Paul's mission. He compared their generosity to *"a fragrant offering"* (4:18 NIV). The backdrop was Leviticus—offerings on the altar.

But another Old Testament image loomed in the background as well. On certain offerings, the law called for oil and wine to be added to the sacrifice (see Exodus 29:40). Along with the sacrifice (in Exodus 29:40 it was a lamb), the priest poured out a "drink offering." In Philippians 2:17, Paul imported that old covenant term—drink offering—and applied it to himself. Oil and wine: something supplemental. It wasn't the main thing.

Paul was saying that even if death for the cause of Christ was his appointed end, and even if in his death he became nothing more than a supplemental addition to the mission of the Philippian church, he was good with that. Like the oil on the offering, he'd be gone. He got that. And he was ok with it.

What if Jeff doesn't get the job? What if we have to take the house off the market? What if I flub that ministry opportunity and people say, "He's losing it"? Let's take Philippians 2:17 as our cue: *"Even if!"* We see that God can take whatever decision or situation we offer him and deploy it—like the oil and wine on the altar—to the glory of his Son.

It's 3:02 a.m., and the fear tries to muscle its way into Paul's mind: "What if Rome puts you to death?"

It's 3:03 a.m., and Paul's got an answer: "Even if ... I am glad!"

Pretty hard to scare a man like that.

Thirty-One

Have You Accepted Yourself as Your Own Personal Lord and Saviour?

"But the serpent said ... 'you will be like God ...'"
—Genesis 3:4–5

The wording in that chapter title is not a typo. It's a straight-up question. It's a riff, of course, on the evangelical catchphrase for placing one's faith in Christ: accepting him as "my own personal Lord and Saviour." I'm asking if you've accepted yourself as that. Whoever you are, the answer is yes. We all have. And that's our problem.

The older and younger brothers in Jesus' "Two Sons" parable (Luke 15) both wanted to be their own Lord and Saviour. They just went about it in different ways. The younger son grabbed oversight of his life away from God and his earthly father and assigned it to himself. He made himself his own Lord. He left home for *"a far country"* (v. 13) and its shallow pleasures (v. 30). That, he thought, would assure him a life worth living. It was how he would be his own Saviour.

The older brother boycotted the welcome-home party. He made himself his own Lord. He *"refused to go in"* (v. 28). He stood jut-jawed on his own virtue: *"Look, these many years I have served you!"* (v. 29). He couldn't respond to the father's invitation. It would cost him his Precious: the thing he cherished most—being his own Saviour.

Unlike the older brother, the younger son *"came to himself"* (v. 17). He relinquished being his own Lord and Saviour. He set out for home, resolved to trustingly surrender to his father—whatever that would mean (v. 19). The old, I-insist-on-writing-my-own-script agenda lost its grip when he took to that road.

In his very helpful book, *The Prodigal God,* Timothy Keller says wanting to be our own Lord and Saviour is the DNA of the fallen self.[27] That distorted identity will do whatever it has to do to avoid simple, humble, child-like, let-the-father-decide-my-fate *trust.* We will scramble and flail to preserve our Lord and Saviour role: striving to have something to show for ourselves, standing jut-jawed on our virtue, longing—misguidedly—for the far country. Or, just as misguidedly, seeing ourselves as God-appointed to set others straight. Or a thousand other inventive ploys. We are creative.

Remember Luke's lead-in to this famous parable: *"Now the tax collectors and sinners were all drawing near to hear him. And the Pharisees and the scribes grumbled, saying, 'This man receives sinners and eats with them'"* (Luke 1:1–2). Coming to that table was how the tax collectors moved toward the real Lord and Saviour (Luke 15:1–2)—and found the treasure.

The younger son in the parable, in coming to the father's party, took the same step.

Urgent good news for judgemental scribes and pious older brothers: the door to that party is still open.

Thirty-Two

The Fourth Man Was with Them

"And he got into the boat with them . . ."

—Mark 6:51a

It's an overlooked gem in a Bible story every Sunday school child knows: the three young men in the fiery furnace. Angry King Nebuchadnezzar ordered Shadrach, Meshach, and Abednego thrown into the flames. But moments later, he stood amazed: *"Look! I see four men walking around in the fire, unbound and unharmed, and the fourth looks like a son of the gods"* (Daniel 3:25, NIV).

The king had reason to be amazed. The three young men were in the midst of the fire, *"unbound and unharmed."* And a mysterious fourth man had appeared. The fourth man was different. He looked like *"a son of the gods."* Was he an angel? Or maybe Christ himself?

Preachers, children's-church teachers, and parents leading family devotions often spin this story to focus on the three men being *"unbound and unharmed."* And rightly so. That was the miracle. But it isn't the overlooked gem. Here's the gem: The men weren't standing still. They were *"walking around in the fire."* Amid the flames, they kept moving. Hard, harsh seasons can immobilize us. We sit. We sigh. We go passive. Not so these three.

During the Second World War, Dutch sisters Corrie and Betsy ten Boom led Bible studies with their fellow inmates at Ravensbrück concentration camp. Caged by barbed wire, guarded by soldiers, guns, and dogs, and surrounded by disease and death, they prayed for the sick and shared the gospel. Like the young men in Daniel, they kept moving. They reflected God in that horrible place. How did they keep moving? They knew the Fourth Man was with them.

In the summer of 2017, Joni Eareckson-Tada marked half a century in a wheelchair. For fifty years she's travelled, published books, and encouraged thousands of people. Paralyzed from the neck down in a diving accident, she's kept moving. One supremely everyday moment from those fifty years occurred when Joni visited England during my time there and spoke one afternoon to a large church audience. Mid-message, she had to pause her talk to change her leg-bag. It was all discreet, unruffled, and done with a touch of humour. Minutes later, she was back on stage. In the face of limitations that would have kept most of us self-conscious, homebound, depressed, and passive, Joni has kept moving.

Shadrach, Meshach, Abednego, Corrie, Betsy, and Joni: six people widely separated by time and place, but with something in common. They all chose to keep moving.[28] They knew the Fourth Man was with them. He was their enabling—and their treasure.

Thirty-Three

We Can Be Like a Tree

"The righteous ... grow like a cedar ..."

—Psalm 92:12

The book of Psalms begins with a hope-birthing promise: We can be like a tree.

"Blessed is the man...[whose] delight is in the law of the Lord, and on [whose] law...he meditates day and night. He is like a tree planted by streams of water that yields its fruit in its season" (Psalm 1:1–3a). Like a tree next to a river: stable (*"planted"*), refreshed (*"by streams of water"*), and full of life (yielding *"its fruit"*). Stability, refreshment, and life: what God promised to those who slowly, deeply pondered—that is, meditated on—the law.

Recall that in the Bible, "the law" usually referred to more than commands-lists (like the Ten Commandments in Exodus 20). It normally applied to the entire five books of Moses: Genesis, Exodus, Leviticus, Numbers, and Deuteronomy. It was commands-lists, histories, songs, genealogies, and more. Five books that formed a unified whole and told a continuous story—with God as the hero. That was the law.[29]

Think about the law and the story that it told. Step back and see how the dots connect. You might come up with something like this:

1. Genesis: God created the whole world and raised up Israel to bless all the nations. He was *global*.

2. Exodus: God brought Israel out of Egypt and drew them to himself at Sinai. He was a *rescuer*.

3. Leviticus: Forty-one times in twenty-seven chapters, Leviticus refers to "the tent of meeting." Global, a rescuer—and ready to meet us. God was *knowable*.[30]

4. Numbers: Sin-based setback: a forty-year wilderness wander! But in that wilderness, God granted water for the thirsty (20:11), and healing for the sick (21:8–9). The global, rescuer, knowable God was *merciful*.

5. Deuteronomy: Early in the law, a loss of place in the eviction from Eden (Genesis 3). At the end of the law, the inheritance of *"a land of grain and wine, whose heavens drop down dew"* (Deuteronomy 33:28b). A new place! God was a *restorer!*

Ponder that story and be that tree: stable, refreshed, full of life. That's what God has promised for those who meditate on the law.

Thirty-Four

The Moving Van Promise

"... in [Christ] are hidden all the treasures ..."

—Colossians 2:3

Velma and I live on the third floor of an old house. For three weeks we've had a racoon in the crawl space above our ceiling. It keeps us up nights with its loud clawing. The ceiling has no access to the crawl space to help us get to the racoon. When I'm joking, I call him Rocky. But I confess I don't always feel like joking.

Amid this medium-size tribulation, I've been pondering God's words to Abram in Genesis 17:7. *"I will ... be God to you, and to your offspring after you."* J.I. Packer called these words the "moving van promise."[26] A moving van, of course, is the big truck that carries everything that belongs to you. Recall house-move day: You finally get the truck loaded. You stand back and think, "Everything that belongs to us is in that van."

In Genesis 17:7, God showed up at Abram's tent with a moving van: "I will be God to you." This one promise carried in itself all God's other promises: blessing on Abram (Genesis 12:2), blessing for the nations (22:18), salvation through Christ (John 8:56). Whatever it meant for God to "be God" (we could ponder that for a hundred lifetimes), God would be that—all that—to Abram. Whatever Abram needed, it was in that van.

And then there's the second half of the promise: "... *and to your offspring after you.*" That is to Isaac, Jacob, and the covenant people that will arise from them. God will be God to them.

Fast forward to the New Testament, to Galatians 3:29: "*And if you are Christ's, then you are Abraham's offspring, heirs according to promise.*" If we are trusting in Christ, we are Abraham's offspring. This means that Genesis 17:7—the moving van promise—belongs to us. Through Christ, God will be God to us.

The pest control people are coming today. No guarantees as to results.

When you're facing stress—a racoon, a job-loss, cancer—what does Genesis 17:7 really mean? It means God exercising his Godness on our behalf. (Note: it's his *God*ness and not just his *good*ness—although it's that too!) It means him doing what he alone can do. It means him ordering our "times" (Psalm 31:15). Abram had to wait many years for Isaac. Velma and I may not be free of Rocky right away. It means him enabling a ninety-nine-year-old barren-all-her-life woman to conceive (Genesis 17:16). And it means him being a "deep calls to deep" life-source: his mighty depths flowing into our needy depths (Psalm 42:7). Into our griefs, our confusions, and our stresses. Into our racoon seasons.

God will be God to us. That is our treasure. Whatever you need today, it's in that van.

Thirty-Five

The God of Again

"I will restore the fortunes of my people . . ."

—Jeremiah 30:3

Several years ago, a close friend of mine suffered a life-alter-ing stroke. It left him with limited speech and reduced use of his right hand. He gamely chose a glass-half-full response and soldiered on—his sense of humour intact. By contrast, I was (on his behalf) shaken and despondent. I couldn't find a solid place to stand.

But soon enough I did find one. I found it in Psalms 42 and 43 (originally a single psalm).[31] They exalted the God of Again: *"My tears have been my food day and night,"* the psalmist said in 42:3a. (Did I mention despondency?) He wistfully recalled happier times: *"These things I remember . . . how I would go with the throng and lead them . . . with glad shouts"* (42:4). That was then, but not now. No glad shouts now.[32]

But there will be: "*O my soul ... Hope in God; for I shall again praise him ...*" (42:5). He repeated these words nearly verbatim in 42:11 and 43:5. He wasn't in "glad shouts" mode yet, but he chose to believe in the God of Again. He knew he'd re-join the throng. Three times he told himself ("*O my soul*") to get ready: "*I shall again praise him.*"

The God of Again: We meet him in creation. Six times Genesis I says, "*And there was evening and there was morning.*" Night, but then day. Darkness, but then dawn. Three-hundred-and-sixty-five times a year, light breaks in. Sunrise is the faithfulness of the God of Again.

We meet him in Israel's post-exile return to the land. Moses saw it coming: God would scatter his people among the nations in judgement (Deuteronomy 28:64). But he would "*gather* [them] *again*" and restore them to the land (30:3). For chronic covenant breakers, the God of Again.

We meet him on the morning of the third day. Jesus was dead. But the God of Again broke in and caused him to "*rise again*" (Mark 8:31b). And note the first-off reason this was good news: "*he is going before you*" (Mark 16:7). Before who? Before those who abandoned him (Mark 14:50). He has not written them off or out of the script. He has risen again, and he will lead them again.

My post-stoke friend moves forward "glass half full." He's able to laugh amid his limits. For my part, I'm rediscovering

the God of again. "Tears" may indeed be "day and night"—
for a season. But not forever. *"Hope in God"* the psalmist told
his soul: *"for I shall again praise him..."* Words declared in the
moment that changed the moment—and can change it again.

Thirty-Six

What Do You Do When You're in a Place That You Can't Leave?

"[Israel] will be sojourners in [Egypt] . . . four hundred years."
—Genesis 15:13

A group of Paul's letters are called the Prison Epistles: Ephesians, Philippians, Colossians, and Philemon. Paul made repeated reference in these books to his "imprisonment," to himself as a "prisoner," and to his "chains" (hence the label). He probably wrote them during his two-year house-arrest in Rome (Acts 28:30–31). The authorities seem to have allowed Paul to receive visitors but not to leave the house.[33]

What do you do when you're in a place that you can't leave? A prison cell? A mind-numbing job? A roommate-group you feel trapped in? A wheelchair? A conflicted family? A friend of mine (I'll call her Joyce) told me about a turn-the-corner moment she'd had on an overseas mission trip. Relational frictions in the team were making for a tense, uphill experience.

Exasperated, she phoned home: "What do I do?" Dad's wise answer was a question: "Joyce, whose prisoner are you?"

Right away, she saw it. He was reminding her of Paul calling himself a *"prisoner of Christ"* (Ephesians 3:1; Philemon 1). Not just *for* Christ, but *of* Christ! The Lord at God's right hand (Acts 2:33) had recruited Paul (Acts 9:16), and—for two years—assigned him to a place he couldn't leave. Paul learned to look above his jailors and focus on Christ. Joyce needed to do the same. In that place she couldn't leave, she belonged to him.

So if we're in a place we can't leave, what to do? We learn with Paul and Joyce: look above your "place" to Christ, enthroned at God's right hand. Remember: We're his prisoners. This is his story, not ours. For our good and God's glory, Christ places us. The sooner we turn that corner, the sooner we'll rejoice.

. Think about how God wants to use you. The Bible's foremost "prisoner" story isn't Paul in Rome but Joseph in Egypt. Falsely accused of sexual assault (Genesis 39:20), he spent years in an Egyptian prison. But he found the good God in the bad events (Genesis 45:7, 50:20). And in the end, God used him to save thousands of Gentiles from famine (Genesis 41:56–57), fulfilling his bless-the-nations promise to Abraham (Genesis 22:18).

Who knows how God might use you in your place?

Remember Paul's prophetic image of the saints-on-mission: they were incense. God, he said, *"manifests through us the sweet aroma of the knowledge of Him in every place"* (2 Corinthians 2:14, NASB). Incense rising. Worship rising. Faith rising. Hope rising. Where? *"In every place."* Including that place that you can't leave.

Thirty-Seven

What We Can't Handle, He Can

"And he put all things under his feet . . ."

—Ephesians 1:22a

The Gospel of Mark gives us four back-to-back scenes about powerless people meeting God's powerful Son. I'm thinking of Mark's text from 4:35 to 5:43. Mark didn't assign the section a title, but he could have: "What We Can't Handle, He Can."

First: The disciples in a boat in a storm. Not just a storm, but a *"great storm"* (Greek, *mega*). The boat was swamped, and the disciples were terrified. Jesus was asleep (there's a whole book in that) and they woke him, saying, *"Teacher, do you not care that we are perishing?"* (Mark 4:38b).[34] He got up and rebuked the wind and the waves, and there came a *"great calm"* (another *mega*). So it was a great storm and a great calm. What we can't handle, he can.

Second: A man in the grip of demons. His life was a parody of a life. He lived naked among the tombs, self-harming, and crying out in emotional pain. People had tried to control him, but *"No one had the strength to subdue him"* (Mark 5:4b). When Jesus arrived, the demons knew they were outmatched. They begged him to cast them into a nearby herd of pigs. He did. The demonized herd rushed into the sea and drowned. Soon after, the long-tormented man was sitting at Jesus' feet, *"clothed and in his right mind"* (Mark 5:15). The contrast couldn't have been starker: The neighbours' futile chain-efforts, and Jesus' authority. What we can't handle, he can.

Third: A woman with a hemorrhage. She'd suffered with it for twelve years and seen all the doctors and found no help. (Panicked storm-rowers, failed demoniac-handlers, unsuccessful doctors: Was there a pattern here?) The woman's condition had left her ritually unclean and in a state of social and ceremonial exile. But her twelve-year disappointment was eclipsed by the instantaneous healing she found in Jesus. All she had to do was touch his garment, and she was well. What we can't handle, he can.

Fourth: Heartbroken parents. Jairus came to Jesus and pled with him to come to his house and heal his near-death daughter. Then Jairus's servants arrived with crushing news—the girl had died—and polite advice: *"Why trouble the Teacher any further?"* (Mark 5:35b). In the servants' minds, the girl was beyond the reach even of Jesus' authority. They were wrong, of course. He went to the house and took her lifeless hand: *"Little girl, I say to you, arise"* (v. 41b). And she did.

What we can't handle, he can.

In these four scenes, the gospel lived in those six words. Whatever your battles are today—especially where you feel powerless—embrace them. They're the treasure.

Thirty-Eight

Ruling What Can't Be Ruled

". . . you have given him dominion . . ."

—Psalm 8:6

Ever tried to rule over a school of fish? Or a room of first graders? Or your own chaotic thoughts? The Big Story began with God appointing mankind to rule: "[Let] *them rule over the fish of the sea . . . and over the livestock and over all the earth . . ."* (Genesis 1:26, NASB). And notice the first item on the rule-over list: fish!

This may strike us as odd. Ruling over "livestock" (cattle, sheep, goats)? Sure, we get that. But schools of cod in the north Atlantic? If we're fishing, it's cast the net and hope for the best. We can't make the fish swim into the net. If fishing is ruling, it's ruling something we can't control.

Fast forward from Genesis to the Gospels: In the beginning days of Christ's public ministry, he miraculously enabled his newly recruited disciples to haul in a huge catch of fish (Luke 5:1–11). (Ruling over fish: sound familiar?) And in the wrap-up days to his time on earth? His final, pre-ascension sign? Another miraculous fish-catch (John 21:1–8)! Jesus bookended his public mission with enabling miracles: signs that empowered people to rule over things they couldn't control. Both these scenes began with weary, up-all-night fishermen—and no fish. Both turned around on the obedience of faith: recasting their nets at Christ's command. Both ended with abundant catches.[35]

Back to Genesis: Ruling, it turned out, wasn't just about cod. It was about character. God warned angry, resentful Cain that sin was *"crouching at the door"* and called him to *"rule over it"* (Genesis 4:7). Another "rule" command, but this time it wasn't about animals.

Paul talked about ruling. Believers are meant to *"reign in life"* (Romans 5:17) and to rely on the Holy Spirit to exercise *"self-control"* (Galatians 5:23)—that is, to do what God told Cain to do: rule themselves. Christ came to win us forgiveness for our sins, yes. But he also came to restore us to the Genesis 1:26 mandate, *"Let them rule."* Fish—and our own hearts.

How do we rule what we can't control? First, we do what Peter did: We surrender: *"Master ... at your word I will ..."* (Luke 5:5). We do what Cain would not. And second, we choose the obedience of faith and take the practical, what-the-moment-calls-for step. Peter knew the fish were outside his control, but he took the step and let down the net.

We know the same about the off-the-wall first graders and our equally off-the-wall thoughts and emotions (Psalm 42:5).[36] They're all outside our control. But not outside Christ's. So we act in faith, and we let down the net.

Thirty-Nine

We Are in Him, and He *is* in Us

"... you, O Lord, are in the midst of this people ..."
—Numbers 14:14

Two mighty ideas, incongruous on the surface, but true according to Scripture: we live in God, and God lives in us. Psalm 90 is the oldest psalm. The superscription says Moses wrote it. Its opening line is a prayer: *"Lord, you have been our dwelling place in all generations."* There it is: we are in him. Centuries later, Paul declared: *"In him we live and move and have our being"* (Acts 17:28a). Some 130 times his letters speak of believers being "in Christ."

Yet God is in us: *"I will dwell among the people of Israel and will be their God"* (Exodus 29:45); *"Judah became his sanctuary"* (Psalm 114:2a). Paul told the Colossians that their hope was the indwelling Christ: *"Christ in you, the hope of glory"* (Colossians 1:27b). And Jesus declared, *"You [are] in me, and I [am] in you"*

(John 14:20). There it was: both sides of the mystery in a single verse.

And "mystery" it was. "Mutual indwelling"—the theological name for this doctrine—is not a brain-easy idea. So try a word-picture: a sea-sponge, living on the ocean floor. A sponge is a simple animal that, plant-like, anchors onto an undersea rock. It lives in the sea. The sea is its dwelling place. But simultaneously, the sea lives in the sponge. Ocean water flows through it, bringing oxygen and food (tiny, nutrient-rich organisms). So the sponge is in the sea, and the sea is in the sponge. We live in God, and God lives in us. And this truth is no mere intellectual curio. It is oxygen. And food.

And a weapon. Psalm 90:1 taught Israel to say to God, *"You have been our dwelling place in all generations."* All generations—including those long, grim, slave-tent years.[37] They lived in ragged tents, but God was their dwelling place. For refugee slaves to declare those words was to fight by faith and reclaim their past in the name of their God. It was to deny the slave-tent memories the last word.

Then there is the other side: God lives in us. What was the apostle John's counsel to Christians facing intense opposition to the gospel? To remind them that they were God's dwelling place: *"… he who is in you is greater than he who is in the world"* (I John 4:4b).

Even in our slave-tent seasons, even when we didn't know it, God has been our dwelling place. And even in the midst of choking resistance to our faith, Christ lives in us. Opposition? Yes—but Christ is greater. We are in him, and he is in us. It's not a curio. It's the treasure.

Forty

The Last Breakfast

"The Lord ... raises up all who are bowed down."

—Psalm 145:14

In Genesis 14:17–24, Abram gathered 318 men to stage a daring all-night rescue.

Enemies—Boko Haram style—had abducted Abram's nephew, Lot, and Lot's family and servants. The rescue succeeded. Abram returned the next morning with Lot and his household safely in tow.

Consider the emotional undercurrents of these events. For a brief time, Abram didn't know if he would see his nephew's family again. Was the experience traumatic? Christians in the West often filter stories like this through children's flannelgraph lessons, which means we tame them. Nigerians who've had family members kidnapped by Boko Haram would read Genesis 14 through different eyes. If I'd been in Lot's shoes—or Abram's—I'm sure I would have felt traumatized and maybe in need of counselling for the much-talked-about "PTSD": Post-Traumatic Stress Disorder.

But amid the trauma, there was that mysterious *"priest of God Most High,"* who was also a king—Melchizedek. On Abram's return, Melchizedek came out to meet him and laid on a meal *("bread and wine")*. He refreshed weary, up-all-night Abram with hospitality—breakfast—and with priestly blessing: *"Blessed be Abram by God Most High, possessor of heaven and earth"* (Genesis 14:19b). Later biblical texts saw this whole episode as a God-thing: a sign to point us to Christ, the ultimate Melchizedek (Psalm 110:4; Hebrews 5:9–10).

John Phillips was my father-in-law. He died in 2015, aged ninety-seven. He was a deeply godly man. On December 31, 1945, he returned from the war in Europe, glad to be home but shell-shocked and emotionally scarred. His family could see it; he carried dark thoughts of watching friends die in battle. In 1945 there was no counselling for PTSD. But John was a man of faith. He learned to draw comfort from his Melchizedek. He and his wife raised five God-centred children. He is with his Melchizedek now.

PTSD has been on men's minds at our church recently after our *Conquerors* classes. *Conquerors* is a video series for men looking for victory over pornography. The videos highlight the peril of unresolved childhood trauma: drunk dad beating cowering mom in front of terrified son. They point to helpful strategies like support groups and, even more important, confidence in a good Father: God. Left untended, childhood trauma leads some men to self-medicate through the toxic pseudo-comfort of pornography. The good news is that we don't need pseudo-comfort. If we're battle-weary or memory-scarred, we can let Christ our Melchizedek come to us with nourishment and blessing.

And ponder this: Christ's last recorded meal on earth was not a supper. It was a breakfast. Hosted by himself (John 21:12).

The morning meal: lead-in to a new day.

About the Author

David Perry has lived and worked in the United States, Canada, and England. He has served in youth ministry and the service sector, and for twenty-one years was a Bible school lecturer. He's the author of *The Cross* (Oxford: Roots and Shoots Books, 1997), and *Why Jesus is Good News: The Gospel of Mark and the Coming of God* (Belleville: Essence Publishing, 2002). David married Velma in 1973. They live in Winnipeg, Canada and have two grown children and four grandchildren. He posts on Facebook at "Dave's Posts" and on Twitter (@frododaveperry). He can be reached on email at daveperry412@gmail.com. His passions are Big Story theology (the Bible as a single story) and seeing the glory of God in all things.

Endnotes

1   J.R.R. Tolkein, *The Lord of the Rings: One Volume 50th Anniversary Edition* (London: HarperCollins, 2005).

2   For those with a mind to check out this scene, and who have a copy of *Monte Cristo* in hand, the treasure scene is at the end of Chapter Twenty-Four.

3   "Clay" in 2 Corinthians 4:7 translates the Greek adjective "earthen" (*ostrakinois*). For Paul, we are all like Adam, whom God formed of *"dust from the ground"* (Genesis 2:7; Psalm 103:14). That is, from the earth.

4   See *The Count of Monte Cristo* by Alexandre Dumas (1844). This was the first novel I ever read (in a youth version) and part of what gave me a love of reading. The plot revolves around injustice and vengeance. The original novel is long and sometimes slow but still very dramatic. The book has provoked mixed reactions from Christians, since some feel it legitimizes revenge.

5   Derek Kidner, *Psalms 1-72: An Introduction and Commentary on Books I and II of the Psalms* (London, Inter-Varsity Press: 1973), 113.

6   Seeing Christ in Psalm 24 is similar to seeing him, as Paul does, in Psalm 66:18 (see Ephesians 4:8). See also Patrick Henry Reardon, *Christ in the Psalms* (Ben Lomond, CA: Conciliar Press, 2000), 47–48. Revelation 4 and 5 give a dramatic picture of heaven worshipping—cheering for—the victorious Lamb.

7   The passage quoted in Luke 4:18 is Isaiah 61:1. Even a cursory reading of the two passages reveals significant differences in what they say. The Luke text quotes Isaiah 61 as it reads in the Greek version of the Old Testament, the Septuagint. For a helpful introduction to the Septuagint and its relationship to the Hebrew Old Testament, see "What is The Septuagint?" by Ryan Reeves, available on The Gospel Coalition website, *The Gospel Coalition.org.* (or go to https://www.thegospelcoalition.org/article/what-is-the-septuagint/).

8   The Bible makes multiple approving references to believers taking risks. I count seven: Judges 5:18, 9:17; 2 Samuel 23:17; 1 Chronicles 11:19; Acts 15:26; Romans 16:4, and Philippians 2:30.

9   J.B. Phillips, *The New Testament in Modern English* (New York: Touchstone, 1995). "Change your hearts and minds" is

Phillips' helpful paraphrase of the Greek *metanoiete* in Mark 1:15— usually translated "repent." Repentance here meant a change in direction, a turning, recalling Old Testament texts like Isaiah 31:6, 45:22, and 59:20. And that turning would begin, of course, in the heart and mind: a change in thinking.

10 ESV translates Romans 8:6 this way: "For to set the mind on the flesh is death, but to set the mind on the Spirit is life and peace." An alternative rendering (which I think better represents the Greek) would be "For the flesh's way of thinking is death, but the Spirit's way of thinking is life and peace." Paul is contrasting two ways of thinking—or two hats! I am indebted for this reading of the Greek to James Dunn, *The Theology of Paul the Apostle* (Cambridge: Eerdmans, 1998), 65, 125.

11 Ecclesiastes is a fascinating and challenging book. It delights in God's goodness and it squarely faces life's pain. Much of the book's teaching flows from the narrative picture of Genesis 3:17–19. This scene describes the eviction from Eden, the futility of human work (sweat, thorns, etc.), and the inescapability of death ("to dust you shall return"). These themes (futility and death) recur throughout Ecclesiastes. It testifies to the frustrating nature of life in a post Genesis 3 world. But Ecclesiastes is nonetheless a life-affirming book. See, for example,

passages like 2:24–26, 5:18–20, 8:15, and 12:9–14. The famous opening refrain, "Vanity of vanity ... All is vanity!" (or, futility, or even vapor, depending on translation) is a key theme but definitely *not* the book's whole message. Ecclesiastes serves us well by reminding us that our frustrations (recall Romans 8:20)—while frustrating! —are part of living in a fallen world, and therefore in a certain sense *make* sense. The book shows us that we are under no obligation to attain to a starry-eyed, endlessly happy-clappy view of life. For a very pastoral and non-technical engagement with the book, see Carolyn Mahaney's brief article (just two-and-a-half pages) "Every Day Is a Bad Day: How Ecclesiastes Taught Me to Enjoy Life," available on the Desiring God website: https://www.desiringgod.org/articles/every-days-a-bad-day.

12   Timothy Keller, *Walking with God through Pain and Suffering* (New York: Penguin, 2013), 279. Keller is speaking about Job himself and his experience as told in the book that bears his name. Keller credits Job commentator Francis Andersen with the phrase "enlarged life with God."

13   For a helpful study of laments, see Stacey Gleddiesmith, "'My God, My God, Why?': Understanding the Lament Psalms," available online at https://www.reformedworship.org/article/june-2010/my-god-my-god-why. Gleddiesmith describes the structure of laments slightly

differently than I do here, but the underlying idea is the same. This is a helpful article, not least due to the author's testimony of how God used the lament psalms in her own life.

14 On "Doe of the Dawn" see brief discussion in Derek Kidner, *Psalms 1–72: An Introduction and Commentary on Books I and II of the Psalms* (London: Inter-Varsity Press, 1973), 41. The notation is variously understood as a melody tag ("To the tune of …") or a thematic note, anticipating the hope-theme in the song's final eleven verses. "Dawn" was an image in the Psalter for new beginnings, or hope: Cf. Psalm 30:5 and 46:5.

15 Not all interpreters see the why-cry as a signal. Some ask whether seeing the cry this way makes the moment seem staged and inauthentic. Another debate-point concerns whether Jesus was (as I claim here) quoting Psalm 22:1 as a pointer to the rest of the psalm, or simply as a godly way to give voice to his anguish. My approach is not to ponder what Jesus could have or would have been "feeling" in this solemn and horrible hour. Rather, it is to read the why-cry in light of what Jesus had said prior to the moment about his impending suffering. The danger of reading the scene strictly through the "Why?" is that it can obscure what Jesus had said earlier about this appointed moment. Mark's account in particular highlights

that Jesus knew well in advance that the suffering was coming, and that it was part of his mission (8:31, 9:31, 10:32). He said his death would be a ransom (10:45). He knew he would experience the judgment of God (the "striking" in 14:27). He knew he would die at Passover (14:14) and would himself become the ultimate Passover sacrifice (14:22). He also believed God would vindicate him by raising him on the third day (8:31, 9:31, 10:32), and that his work would be "proclaimed in the whole world" (14:9). The why-cry of Mark 15:34, then, did not mean he did not know what was going on. It meant he *did* know: He was dying to fulfill Psalm 22—that mighty, hope-filled hymn that Israel had been singing for a thousand years. It began in anguish ("Why?") but ended with the nations turning to God (v. 27). For a detailed academic study of the "why-cry" and how it connects with the full sweep of Psalm 22, see Holly Carey, *Jesus' Cry from the Cross: Towards a First-Century Understanding of the Intertextual Relationship between Psalm 22 and the Narrative of Mark's Gospel* (London: T & T Clark, 2009).

16 C.S. Lewis, *Reflections on the Psalms* (New York: Harper One, 1958), 73–74.

17 Gerard Manley Hopkins, *God's Grandeur and Other Poems* (New York: Dover Publications, 1995), 15.

18 Mark 1:10 and 15:38 both use the same verb, *schidzo*, meaning rip or tear. The two verses are the only times Mark employed this verb, suggesting that he intended the reader to infer a link between them. For a helpful study of the theological link between the two tearings (Mark 1:10 and 15:38), see David Ulansey, "The Heavenly Veil Torn: Mark's Cosmic Inclusio," *Journal of Biblical Literature* 110 [1991]: 123–25).

19 Google "International Justice Mission" or go to the IJM website at https://www.ijm.org/our-work.

20 J.R.R. Tolkien, *The Lord of the Rings: Fiftieth Anniversary, Single-Volume Edition* (London: HarperCollins, 2005), 170.

21 G.E. Veith, *God at Work: Your Christian Vocation in All of Life* (Wheaton: Crossway Books, 2002), 1. For more on God's intended role for our work, see Timothy Keller's excellent study, *Every Good Endeavor: Connecting Your Work to God's Work* (New York: Penguin Books, 2012).

22 In Scripture, Christ being physically *born* was more than a sentimental, Christmas-card idea. He was more than a divine being appearing in human form—like the "men" in Genesis 18 who were in fact angels. Those heavenly messengers appeared temporarily on earth as men but did not literally join the human race, as God's Son did: "For to us a *child* is *born*" (Isaiah 9:6). The gospel of John and the book of Hebrews both highlight the turning-point

importance of Christ becoming fully human: John 1:14 and Hebrews 2:17.

23 Isaiah 49:1–7 is the second of what are known as the "Servant Songs": See also Isaiah 42:1–9, 50:4–11, and 52:13–53:12. (Some scholars include Isaiah 61 in this group as well.) These poems portrayed an individual commissioned by God to restore the people of Israel and bring justice to all the nations. They also highlighted this "Servant's" suffering (e.g., 49:4 and 52:13–53:12). The New Testament repeatedly referenced these passages as pointing to Christ. For a helpful study of the Servant Songs, see Henri Blocher, *Songs of the Servant: Isaiah's Good News* (Vancouver: Regent College Publishing, 2005).

24 Mark shows the simultaneity of the two scenes by referring 1) to Peter in 14:54, 2) to Jesus in verses 55-65 and then 3) back again to Peter in verses 66-72. By inter-splicing the two scenes in this way Mark stresses the stark contrast between the two men: Peter is lying, but Jesus is speaking the truth.

25 Chronologically, the "Galilee" visit of Mark 16:7 and John 21:1–13 seems to have taken place between Jesus' resurrection and his appearance to the disciples, apparently in or near Jerusalem, in Luke 24:44–49.

26 J.I. Packer, *Knowing God* (Downers Grove: InterVarsity Press, 1973), 114. Packer uses a common British term for moving van, "pantechnicon."

27 See Timothy Keller, *The Prodigal God* (New York: Riverhead Books, 2008), especially chapters two and three.

28 I am indebted in this meditation to chapter three ("Walking") of Timothy Keller, *Walking with God through Pain and Suffering* (New York: Penguin Books, 2013).

29 I am indebted to several scholars for the idea of the Bible's first five books (the "Pentateuch") forming a unified, coherent story. Notably, John Sailhamer, *The Pentateuch as Narrative* (Grand Rapids: Zondervan, 1992) and David J.A. Clines, *The Theme of the Pentateuch* (Sheffield: JSOT Press, 2001), but most of all my Old Testament professor at Providence Theological Seminary, Gus Konkel. He taught us to see the five books of Moses as a coherent story, with a single, central theme—God's covenant with Israel for the sake of the nations. I well recall his booming voice in the lecture hall: "God refused to give up on his world!" The message of the Pentateuch, in eight words.

30 The knowable God personally met with his people, first in the temporary "tent of meeting, which was outside the camp" (Exodus 33:7), and then in the more formal and elaborate "tabernacle" at the center of the camp (Exodus 40, Numbers 2:2). The tabernacle then took on the

name and function of its temporary predecessor, the tent of meeting. The naming of this place of worship in Leviticus is interesting. Leviticus referred to the tabernacle by that name only three times, but by the name "tent of meeting" forty-one times! The point? God wants to *meet* with us! He is knowable!

31 Derek Kidner, *Psalms 1-72: An Introduction and Commentary on Books I and II of the Psalms* (London, Inter-Varsity Press: 1973), 165.

32 Interpreters differ in their reading of the "remembering" in Psalm 42:4 ("These things I remember, as I pour out my soul: how I would go with the throng and lead them in procession …"). Some do not see wistfulness here (as I do) and take this remembering as a choice amid misfortune to recall God's past mercies. The whole point of Psalms 42 and 43 was of course the goodness of God. Three times the psalmist rallied his emotions, saying, "Hope in God" (42:5, 11, and 43:5). The reason I see wistfulness in 42:4 is that it seems to be part of the thought-flow of the lament beginning in verse three ("My tears have been my food …"). Seen this way, 42:4 is like the poignant remembering of Psalm 137:1: "By the waters of Babylon, there we sat down and wept, when we remembered Zion". Still—and importantly— the

double psalm (42 and 43 together) went on to declare, three times: "I shall again praise him" (42:5,11, 43:5).

33 See, for example, Paul's mention of "imprisonment" in Philippians 1:7,13,14,17; Philemon 10 and 13. Also his self-reference as a "prisoner" in Ephesians 3:1, 4:1, Colossians 4:10, and Philemon 1, 9, 23. And, further, his mention of his "chains" in Ephesians 6:20 and Colossians 4:18. If we identify the time frame of these texts with the two years mentioned in Acts 28:30–31, we observe that he remained under the guard of soldiers (Acts 28:16; Philippians 1:13), but in his own rented house (Acts 28:30) rather than a literal prison. So though he lived in a house and not a jail, the "guard" detail in Acts 28:16 and biographical references in his letters (just mentioned) all suggest restriction of movement: Paul was in a place he could not leave.

34 The disciples' frightened cry recalled Psalm 44:23: "Awake! Why are you sleeping, O Lord?"

35 "The obedience of faith" is a Paul-term. He bookended Romans with this short, theologically rich phrase: see Romans 1:5 and 16:26. These two verses in Romans are the only places in Scripture that use these exact words. But of course, they represent the message of the whole book of Romans and, to a degree, the message of the whole Bible.

36 Scripture has a fair bit to say about ruling our unruly thoughts. See also Psalm 13:2, 103:1; 2 Corinthians 2:13, 7:5.

37 I am indebted for this insight into Psalm 90 to a poem by Luci Shaw: "Moses: Psalm XC," in Luci Shaw, *Listen to the Green* (Wheaton, IL: Harold Shaw, 1971), 53.